EVERY GIRL IS THE END
OF THE WORLD FOR ME

JEFFREY BROWN

DECEMBER 26 2003 - JANUARY 15 2004

EVERY GIRL IS THE END OF THE WORLD FOR ME
(MOSTLY TRUE STORY, NOT QUITE TRUE TITLE)

ISBN 189 183 0775

PUBLISHED BY TOP SHELF PRODUCTIONS
PO BOX 1282 MARIETTA GA 30061-1282
TOP SHELF PRODUCTIONS AND THE TOP SHELF LOGO ARE
TM AND ©2005 BY TOP SHELF PRODUCTIONS INC.
PRODUCTION BY BRETT WARNOCK AND JEFFREY BROWN

THANK YOU TO ALL OF THE GIRLS IN THIS BOOK
FOR THEIR TOLERANCE, UNDERSTANDING, FRIENDSHIP
AND SUPPORT, IN SPITE OF MY MANY FAULTS,
AND ALSO TO ALL MY FRIENDS, FAMILY AND FANS.

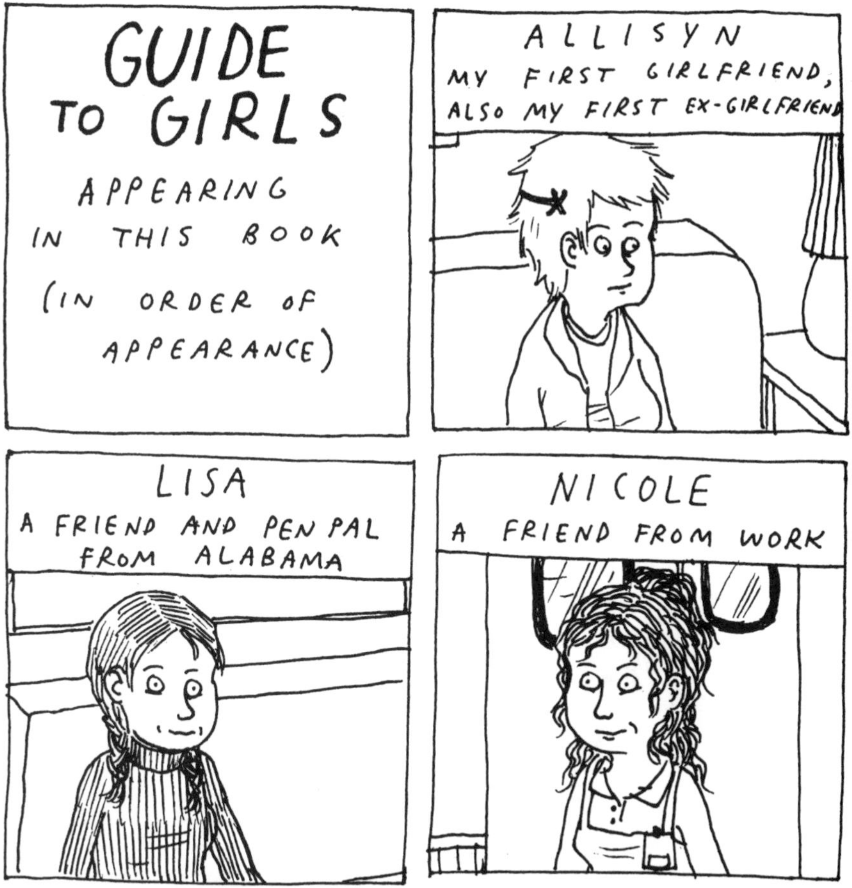
GUIDE TO GIRLS
APPEARING IN THIS BOOK
(IN ORDER OF APPEARANCE)
ALLISYN
MY FIRST GIRLFRIEND, ALSO MY FIRST EX-GIRLFRIEND
LISA
A FRIEND AND PEN PAL FROM ALABAMA
NICOLE
A FRIEND FROM WORK

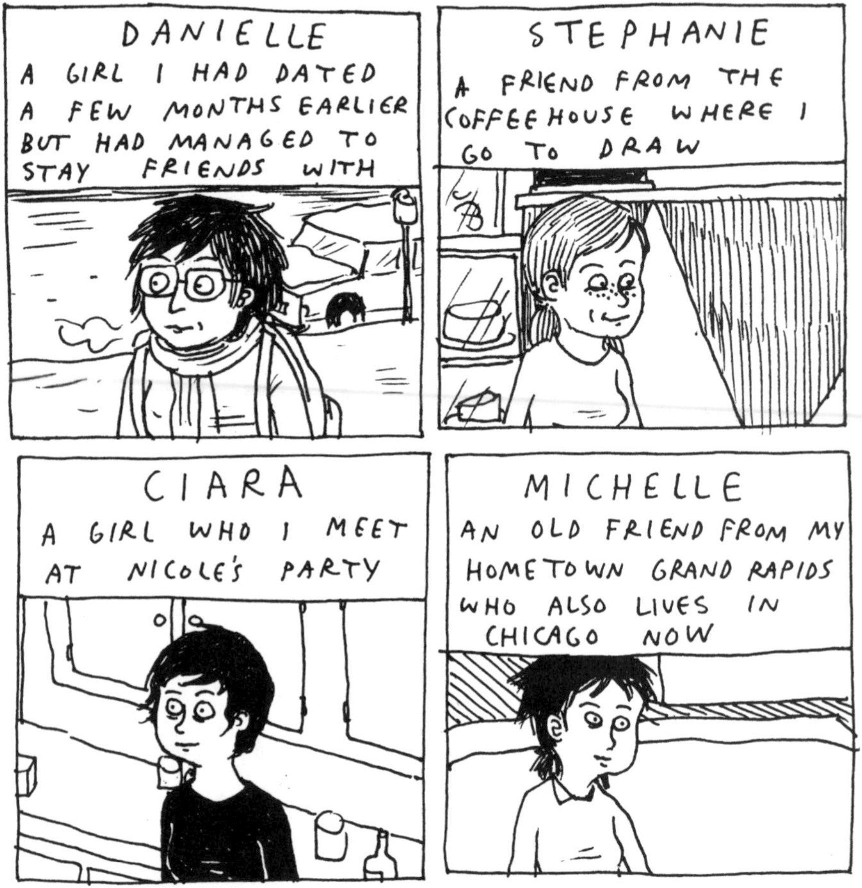
DANIELLE
A GIRL I HAD DATED A FEW MONTHS EARLIER BUT HAD MANAGED TO STAY FRIENDS WITH
STEPHANIE
A FRIEND FROM THE COFFEE HOUSE WHERE I GO TO DRAW
CIARA
A GIRL WHO I MEET AT NICOLE'S PARTY
MICHELLE
AN OLD FRIEND FROM MY HOMETOWN GRAND RAPIDS WHO ALSO LIVES IN CHICAGO NOW

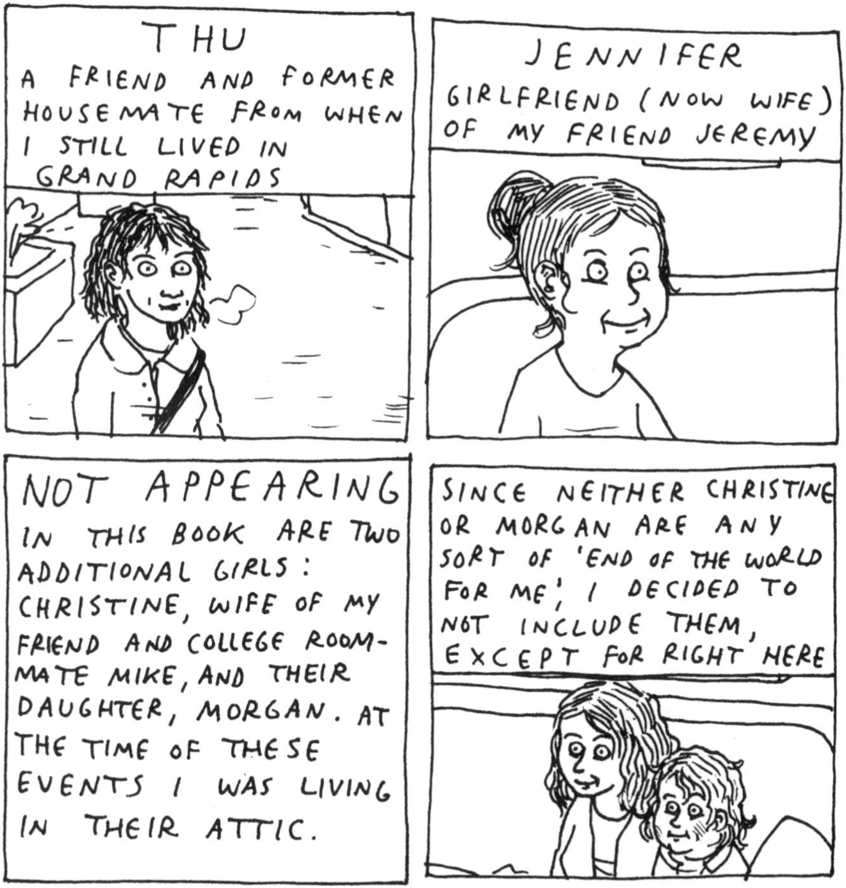
THU
A FRIEND AND FORMER HOUSEMATE FROM WHEN I STILL LIVED IN GRAND RAPIDS
JENNIFER
GIRLFRIEND (NOW WIFE) OF MY FRIEND JEREMY
NOT APPEARING
IN THIS BOOK ARE TWO ADDITIONAL GIRLS: CHRISTINE, WIFE OF MY FRIEND AND COLLEGE ROOMMATE MIKE, AND THEIR DAUGHTER, MORGAN. AT THE TIME OF THESE EVENTS I WAS LIVING IN THEIR ATTIC.
SINCE NEITHER CHRISTINE OR MORGAN ARE ANY SORT OF 'END OF THE WORLD FOR ME', I DECIDED TO NOT INCLUDE THEM, EXCEPT FOR RIGHT HERE

PREVIOUSLY

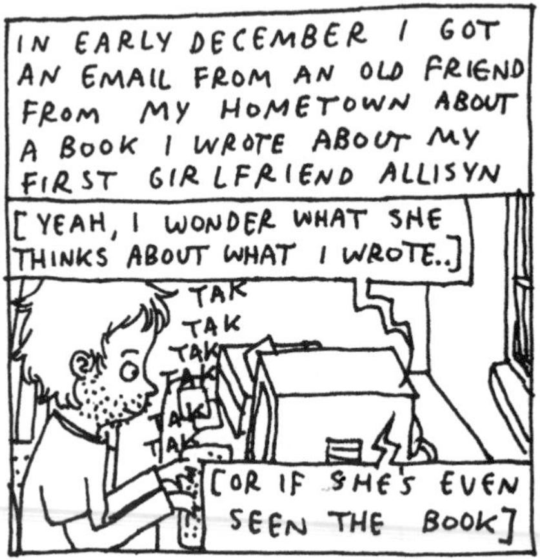
IN EARLY DECEMBER I GOT AN EMAIL FROM AN OLD FRIEND FROM MY HOMETOWN ABOUT A BOOK I WROTE ABOUT MY FIRST GIRLFRIEND ALLISYN
[YEAH, I WONDER WHAT SHE THINKS ABOUT WHAT I WROTE..]
TAK TAK TAK TAK TAK TAK
[OR IF SHE'S EVEN SEEN THE BOOK]

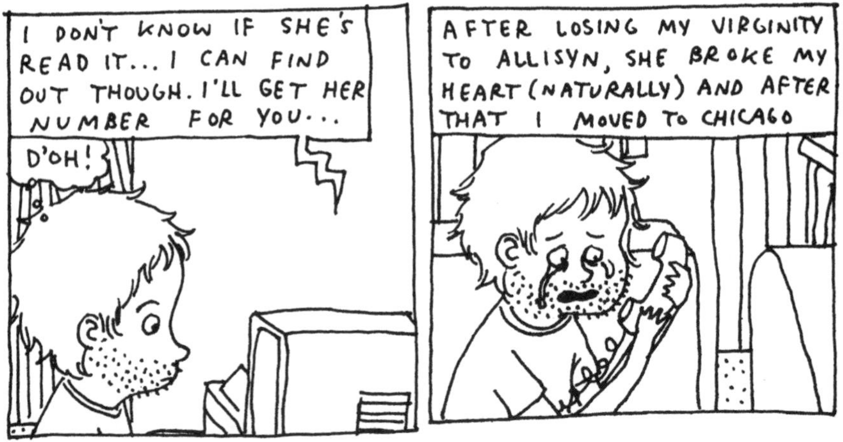
I DON'T KNOW IF SHE'S READ IT... I CAN FIND OUT THOUGH. I'LL GET HER NUMBER FOR YOU...
D'OH!
AFTER LOSING MY VIRGINITY TO ALLISYN, SHE BROKE MY HEART (NATURALLY) AND AFTER THAT I MOVED TO CHICAGO

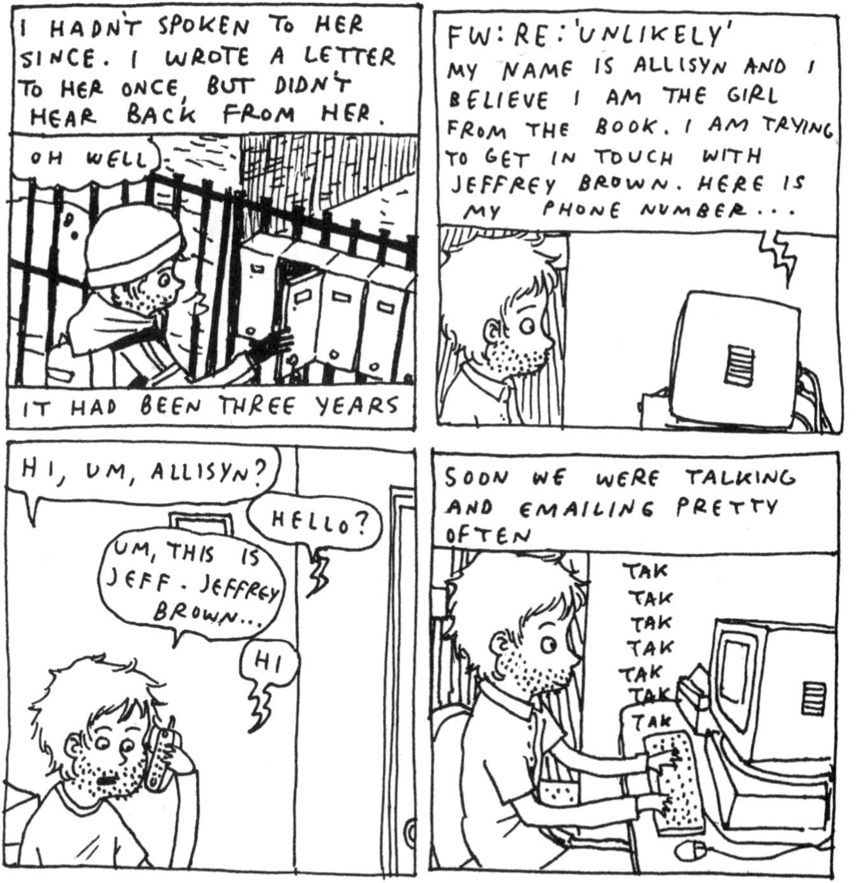
I HADN'T SPOKEN TO HER SINCE. I WROTE A LETTER TO HER ONCE, BUT DIDN'T HEAR BACK FROM HER.
OH WELL
IT HAD BEEN THREE YEARS
FW: RE: 'UNLIKELY'
MY NAME IS ALLISYN AND I BELIEVE I AM THE GIRL FROM THE BOOK. I AM TRYING TO GET IN TOUCH WITH JEFFREY BROWN. HERE IS MY PHONE NUMBER...
HI, UM, ALLISYN?
HELLO?
UM, THIS IS JEFF. JEFFREY BROWN...
HI
SOON WE WERE TALKING AND EMAILING PRETTY OFTEN
TAK
TAK
TAK
TAK
TAK
TAK
TAK

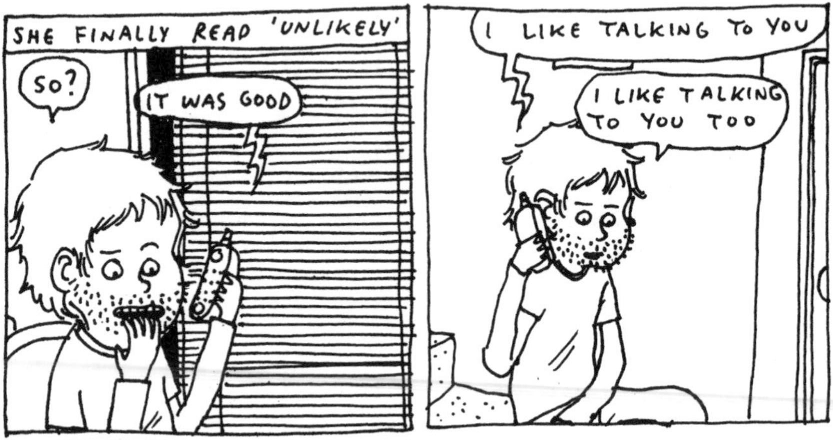
SHE FINALLY READ 'UNLIKELY'
SO?
IT WAS GOOD
I LIKE TALKING TO YOU
I LIKE TALKING TO YOU TOO

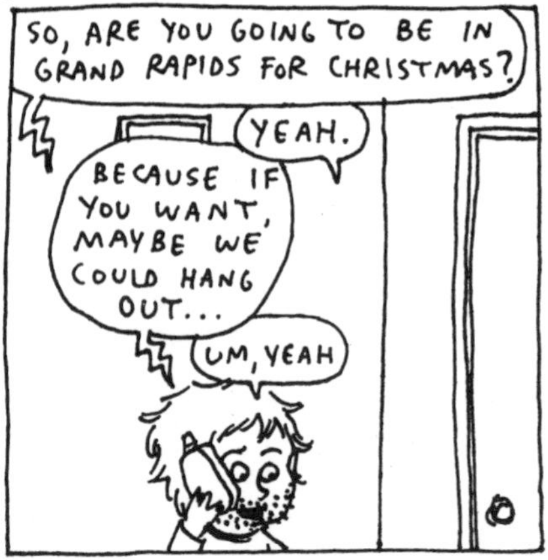
SO, ARE YOU GOING TO BE IN GRAND RAPIDS FOR CHRISTMAS?
YEAH.
BECAUSE IF YOU WANT, MAYBE WE COULD HANG OUT...
UM, YEAH

FRIDAY DECEMBER 26

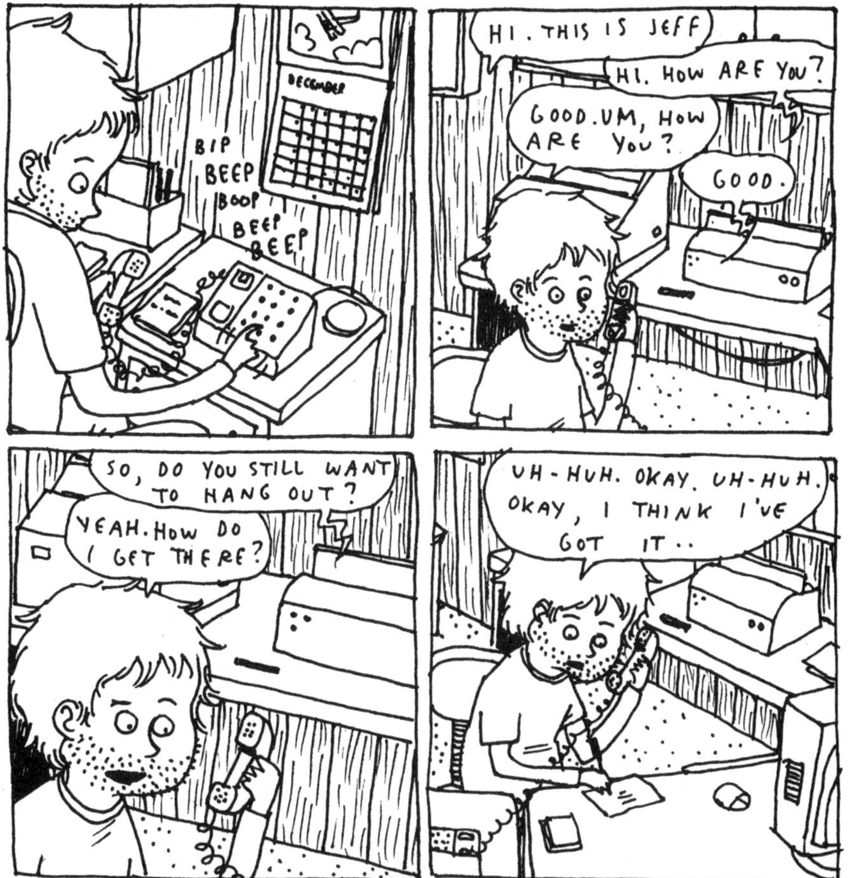
DECEMBER
BIP
BEEP
BOOP
BEEP
BEEP
HI. THIS IS JEFF
HI. HOW ARE YOU?
GOOD. UM, HOW ARE YOU?
GOOD.
SO, DO YOU STILL WANT TO HANG OUT?
YEAH. HOW DO I GET THERE?
UH-HUH. OKAY. UH-HUH. OKAY, I THINK I'VE GOT IT..

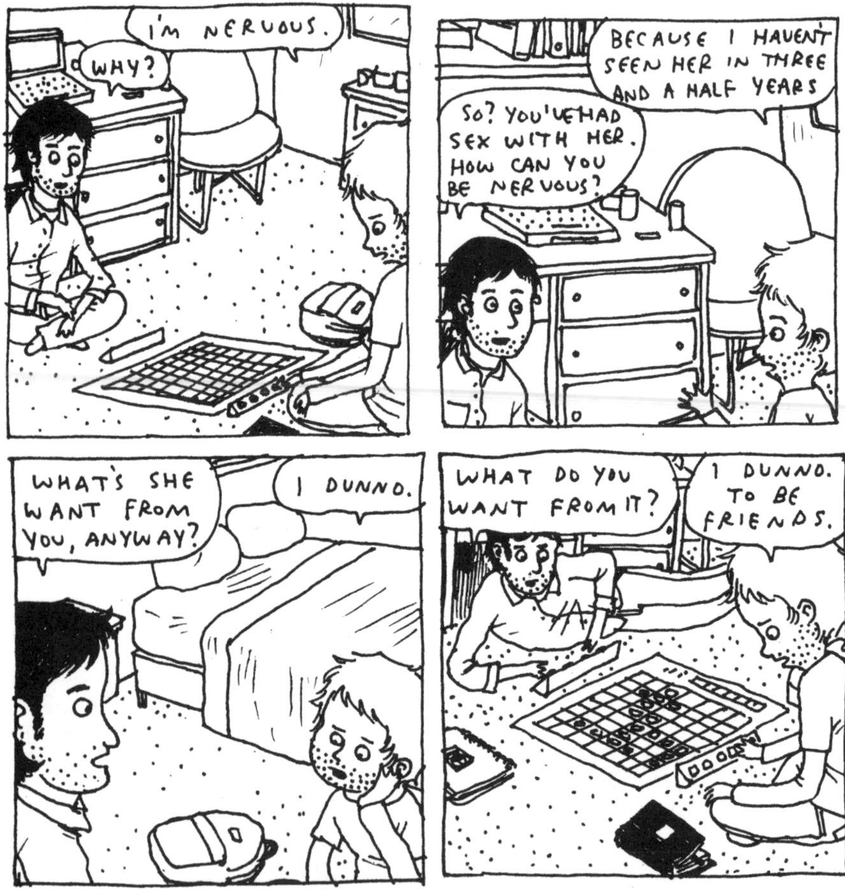
I'M NERVOUS.
WHY?
BECAUSE I HAVEN'T SEEN HER IN THREE AND A HALF YEARS
SO? YOU'VE HAD SEX WITH HER. HOW CAN YOU BE NERVOUS?
WHAT'S SHE WANT FROM YOU, ANYWAY?
I DUNNO.
WHAT DO YOU WANT FROM IT?
I DUNNO. TO BE FRIENDS.

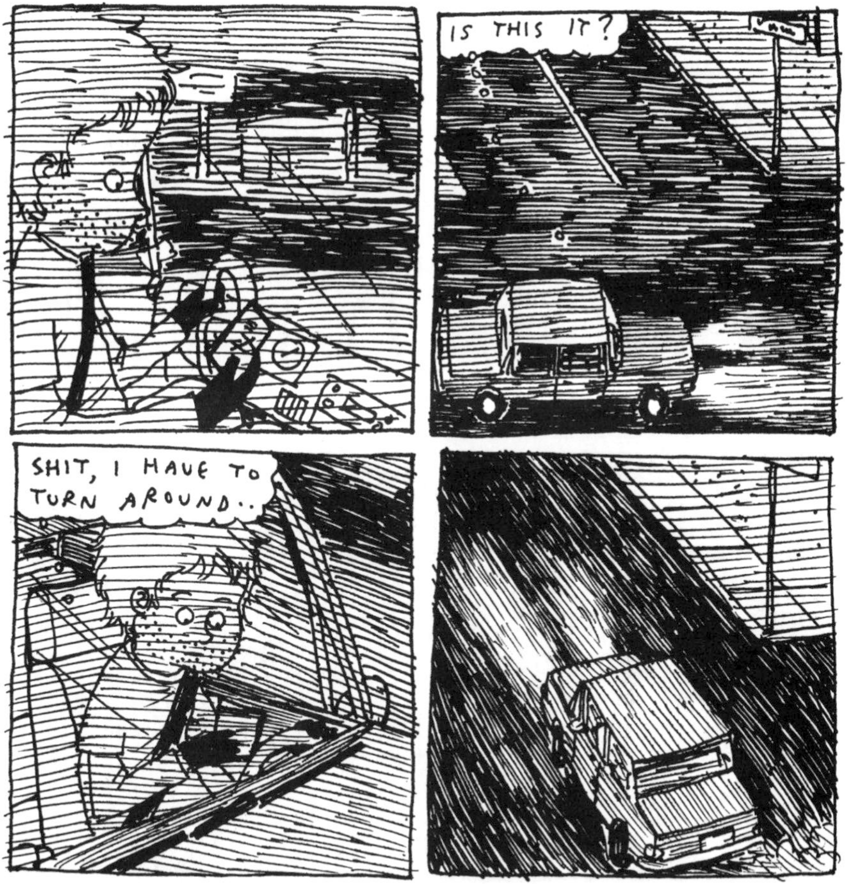
IS THIS IT?
SHIT, I HAVE TO TURN AROUND..

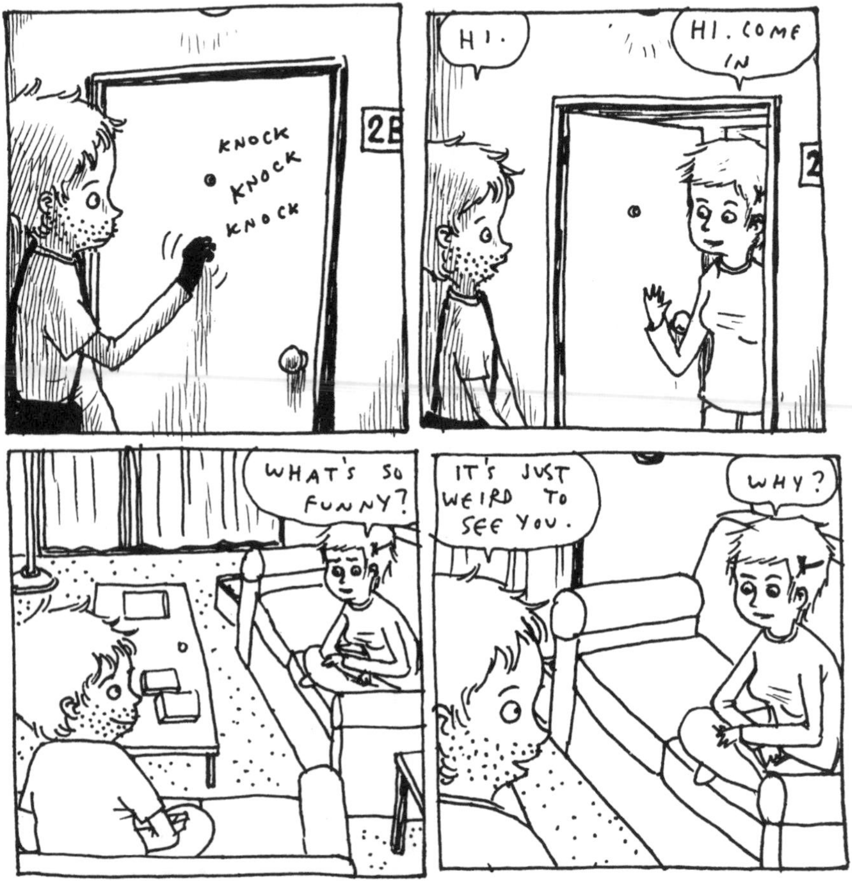
2B
KNOCK
KNOCK
KNOCK
HI.
HI. COME IN
WHAT'S SO FUNNY?
IT'S JUST WEIRD TO SEE YOU.
WHY?

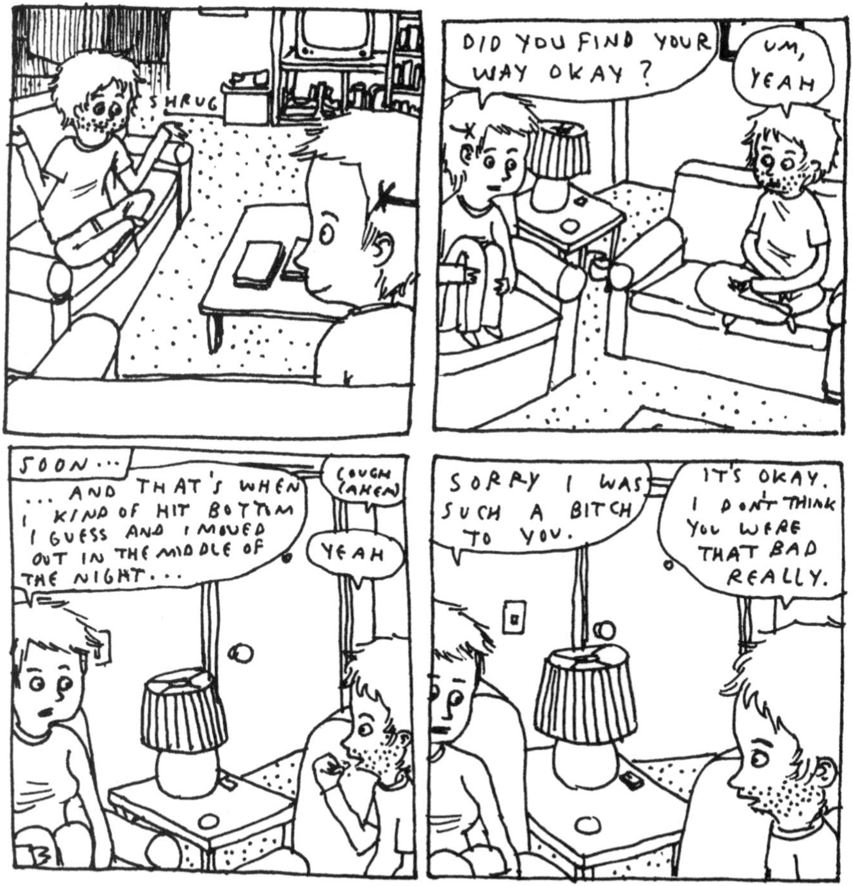
SHRUG
DID YOU FIND YOUR WAY OKAY?
UM, YEAH
SOON...
...AND THAT'S WHEN I KIND OF HIT BOTTOM I GUESS AND I MOVED OUT IN THE MIDDLE OF THE NIGHT...
COUGH (AHEM)
YEAH
SORRY I WAS SUCH A BITCH TO YOU.
IT'S OKAY. I DON'T THINK YOU WERE THAT BAD REALLY.
13

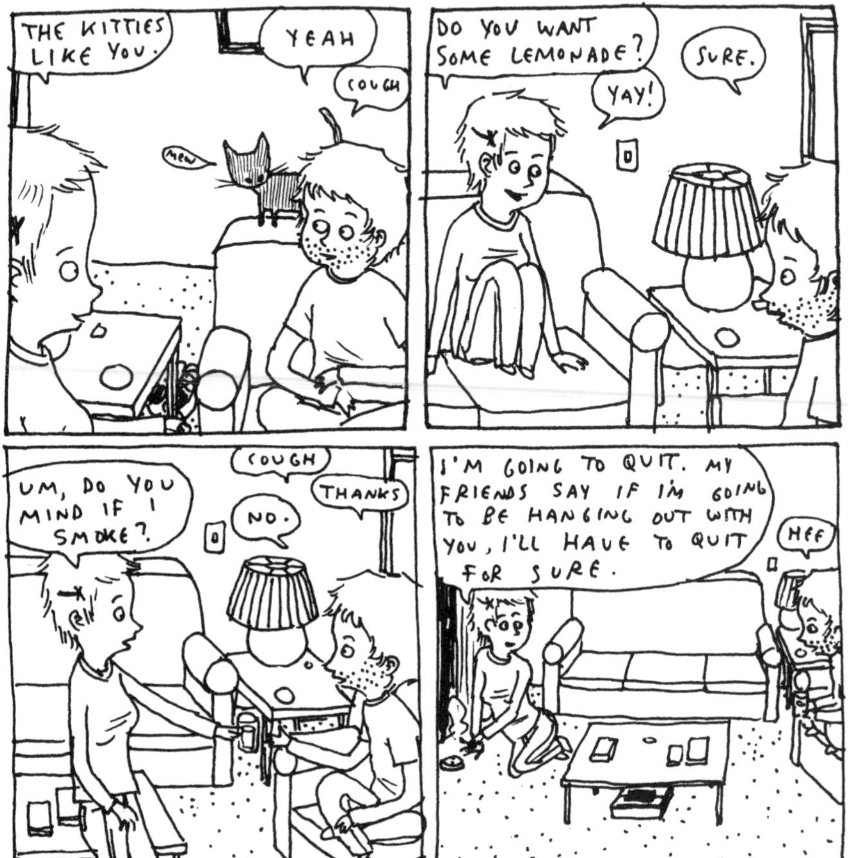
THE KITTIES LIKE YOU.
YEAH
COUGH
MEW
DO YOU WANT SOME LEMONADE?
YAY!
SURE.
UM, DO YOU MIND IF I SMOKE?
COUGH
NO.
THANKS
I'M GOING TO QUIT. MY FRIENDS SAY IF I'M GOING TO BE HANGING OUT WITH YOU, I'LL HAVE TO QUIT FOR SURE.
HEF

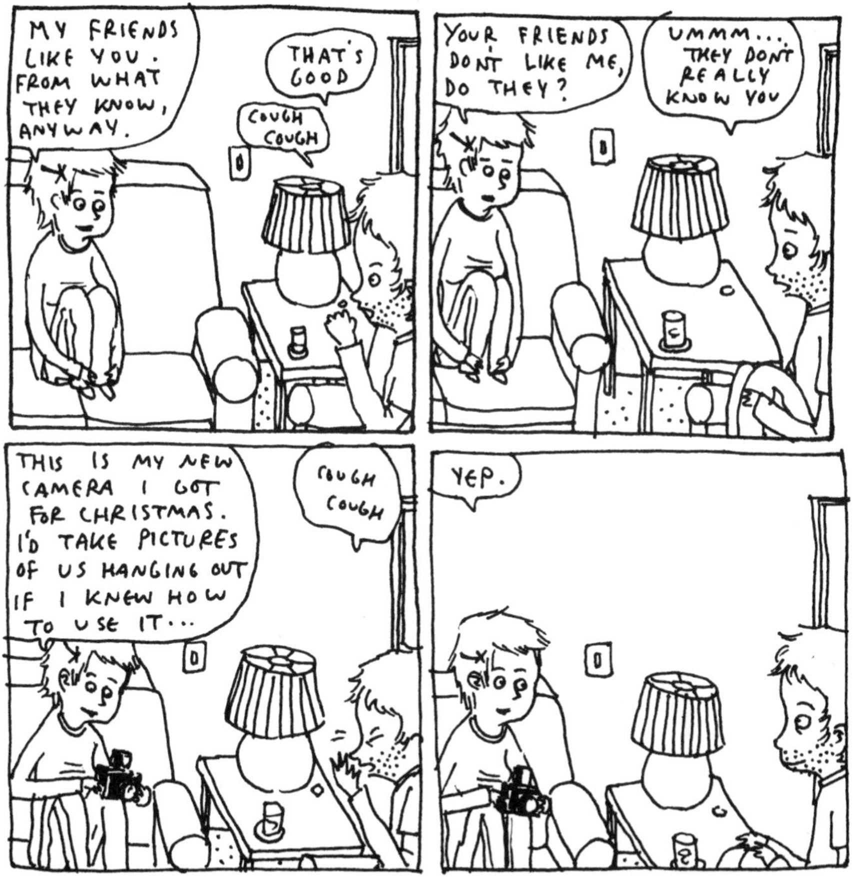
MY FRIENDS LIKE YOU. FROM WHAT THEY KNOW, ANYWAY.
THAT'S GOOD
COUGH COUGH
YOUR FRIENDS DON'T LIKE ME, DO THEY?
UMMM... THEY DON'T REALLY KNOW YOU
THIS IS MY NEW CAMERA I GOT FOR CHRISTMAS. I'D TAKE PICTURES OF US HANGING OUT IF I KNEW HOW TO USE IT...
COUGH COUGH
YEP.

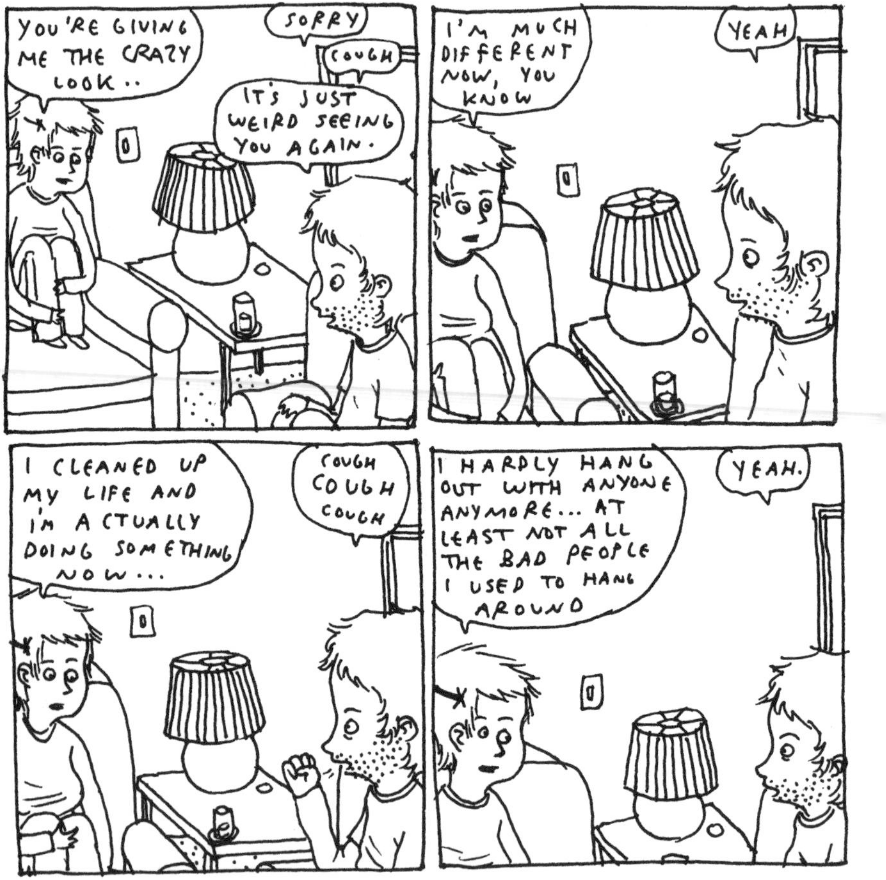
YOU'RE GIVING ME THE CRAZY LOOK..
SORRY
COUGH
IT'S JUST WEIRD SEEING YOU AGAIN.
I'M MUCH DIFFERENT NOW, YOU KNOW
YEAH
I CLEANED UP MY LIFE AND I'M ACTUALLY DOING SOMETHING NOW...
COUGH COUGH COUGH
I HARDLY HANG OUT WITH ANYONE ANYMORE... AT LEAST NOT ALL THE BAD PEOPLE I USED TO HANG AROUND
YEAH.

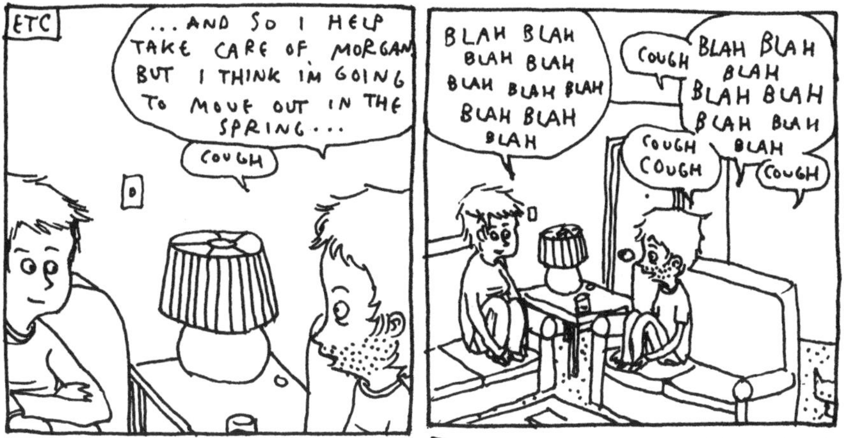
ETC
...AND SO I HELP TAKE CARE OF MORGAN BUT I THINK I'M GOING TO MOVE OUT IN THE SPRING...
COUGH
BLAH BLAH BLAH BLAH BLAH BLAH BLAH BLAH BLAH BLAH
COUGH
BLAH BLAH BLAH BLAH BLAH BLAH BLAH BLAH
COUGH COUGH
COUGH

SATURDAY

DECEMBER 27

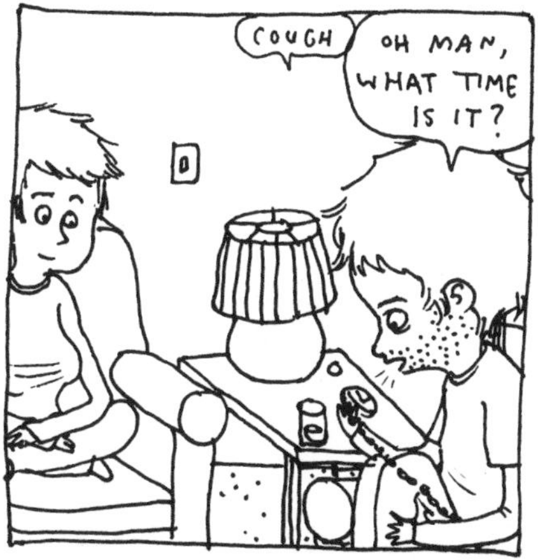
COUGH
OH MAN, WHAT TIME IS IT?

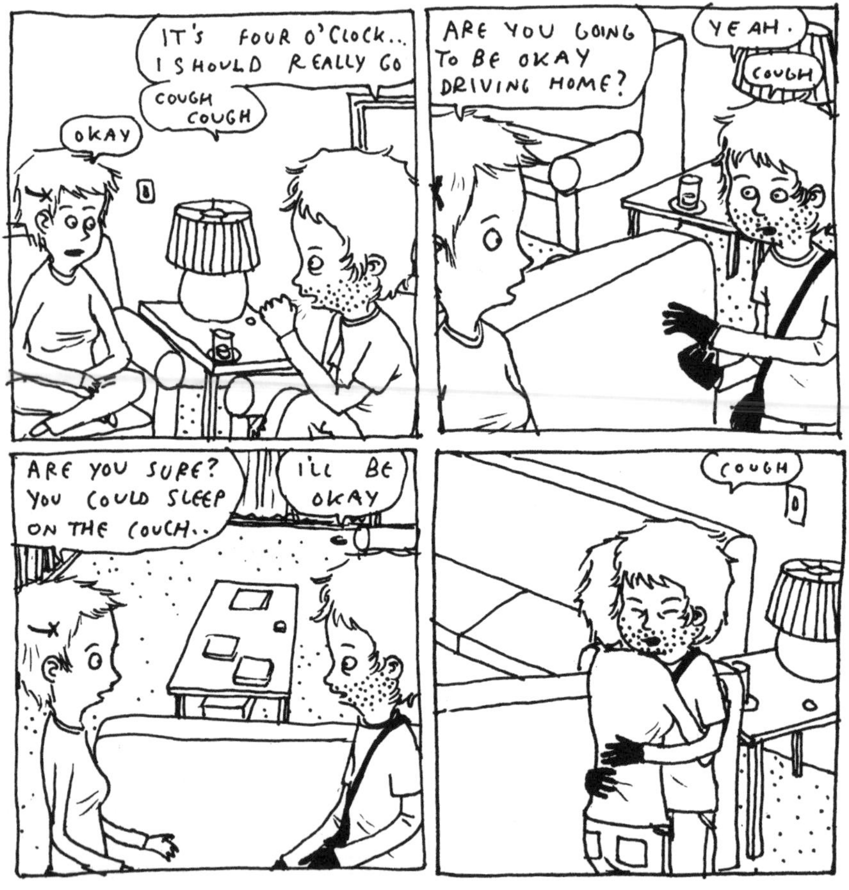
IT'S FOUR O'CLOCK... I SHOULD REALLY GO
COUGH COUGH
OKAY
ARE YOU GOING TO BE OKAY DRIVING HOME?
YEAH.
COUGH
ARE YOU SURE? YOU COULD SLEEP ON THE COUCH..
I'LL BE OKAY
COUGH

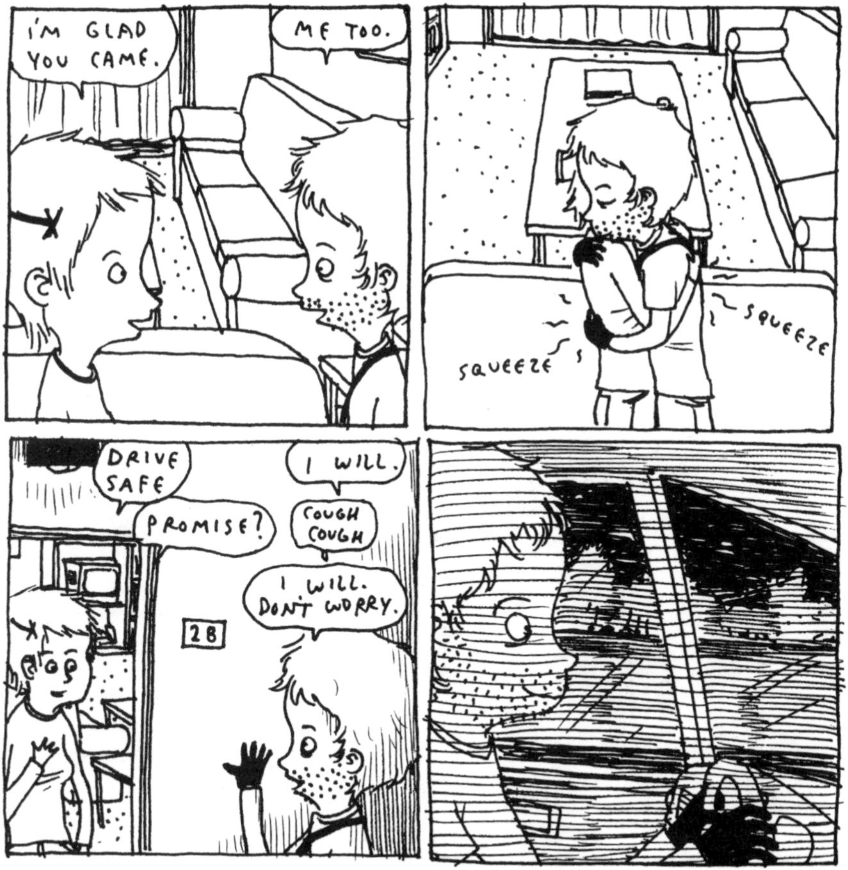
I'M GLAD YOU CAME.
ME TOO.
SQUEEZE
SQUEEZE
DRIVE SAFE
I WILL.
PROMISE?
COUGH COUGH
I WILL. DON'T WORRY.
28

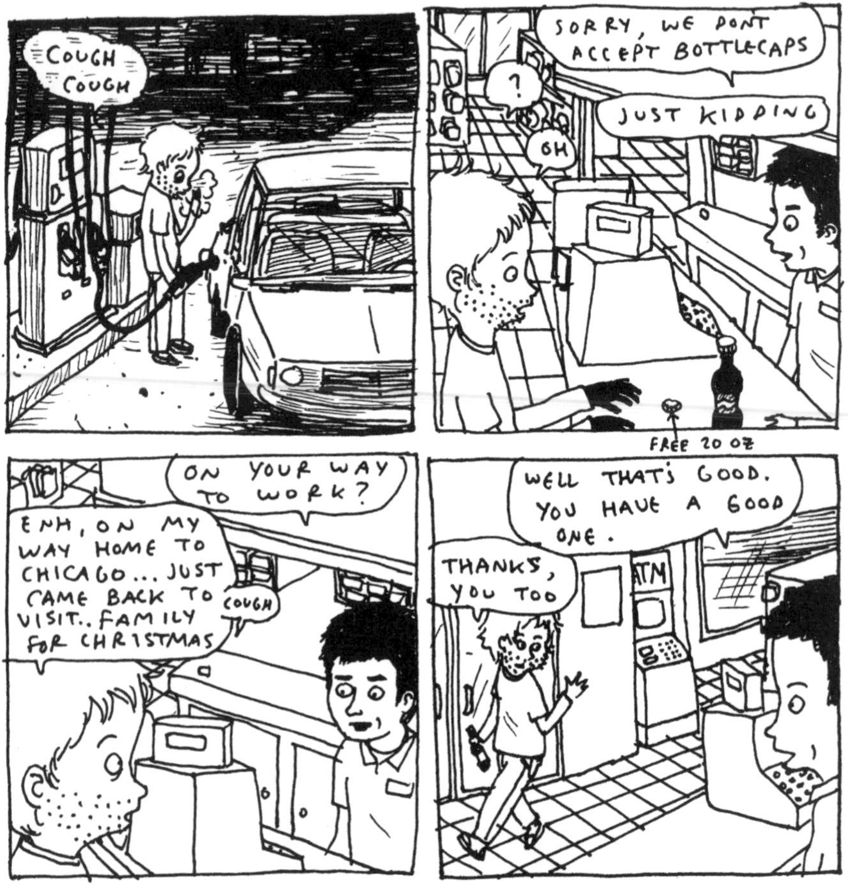
COUGH COUGH
SORRY, WE DONT ACCEPT BOTTLECAPS
?
JUST KIDDING
OH
FREE 20 OZ
ON YOUR WAY TO WORK?
ENH, ON MY WAY HOME TO CHICAGO... JUST CAME BACK TO VISIT.. FAMILY FOR CHRISTMAS
COUGH
WELL THAT'S GOOD. YOU HAVE A GOOD ONE.
THANKS, YOU TOO

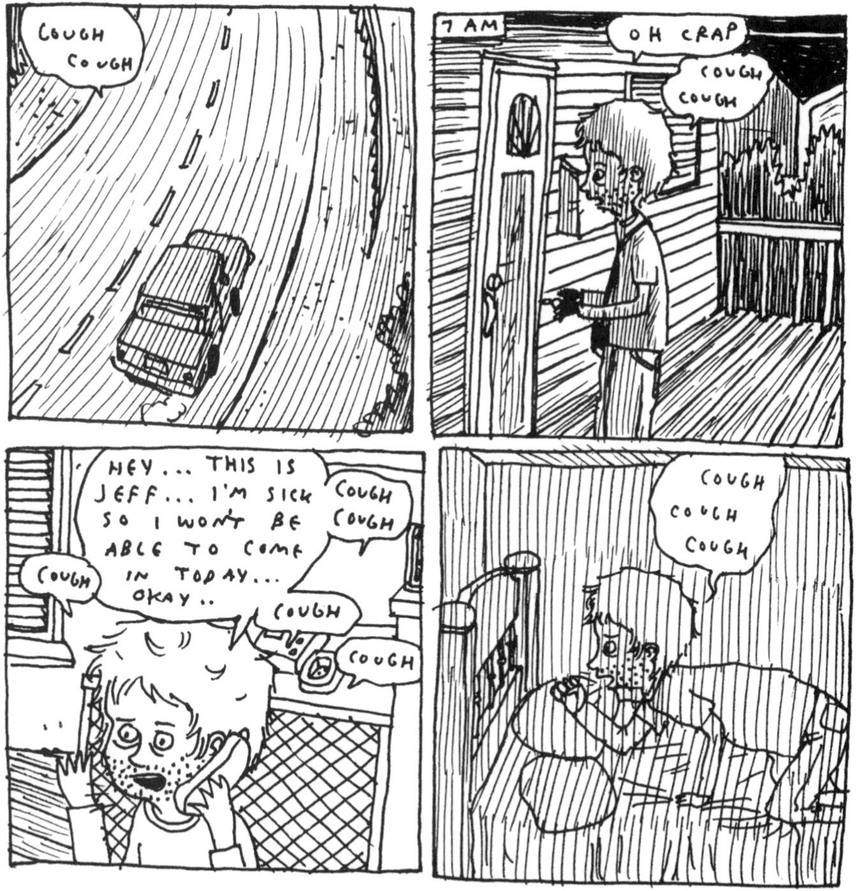
COUGH
COUGH
7 AM
OH CRAP
COUGH
COUGH
HEY... THIS IS JEFF... I'M SICK SO I WON'T BE ABLE TO COME IN TODAY... OKAY..
COUGH
COUGH
COUGH
COUGH
COUGH
COUGH
COUGH
COUGH

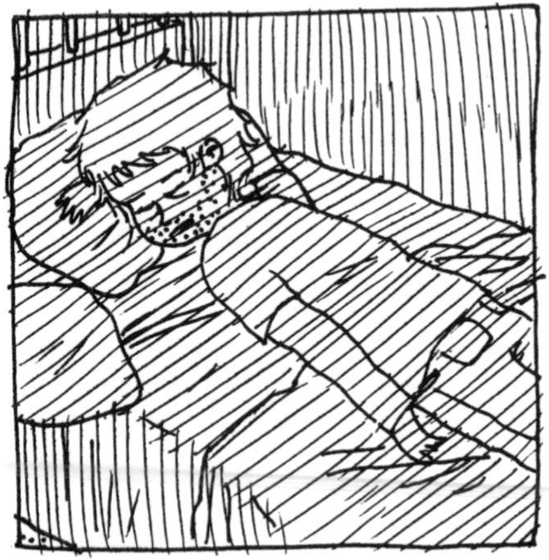

SUNDAY

DECEMBER 28

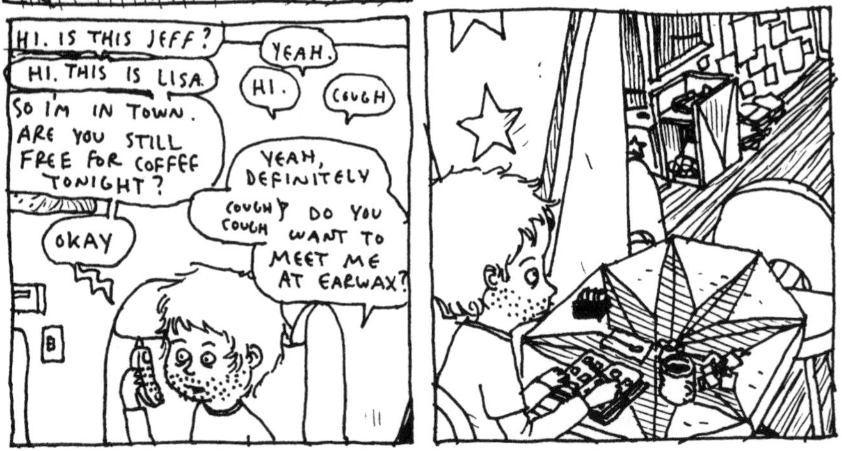
HI. IS THIS JEFF?
YEAH.
HI. THIS IS LISA.
HI.
COUGH
SO I'M IN TOWN. ARE YOU STILL FREE FOR COFFEE TONIGHT?
YEAH, DEFINITELY
COUGH COUGH DO YOU WANT TO MEET ME AT EARWAX?
OKAY

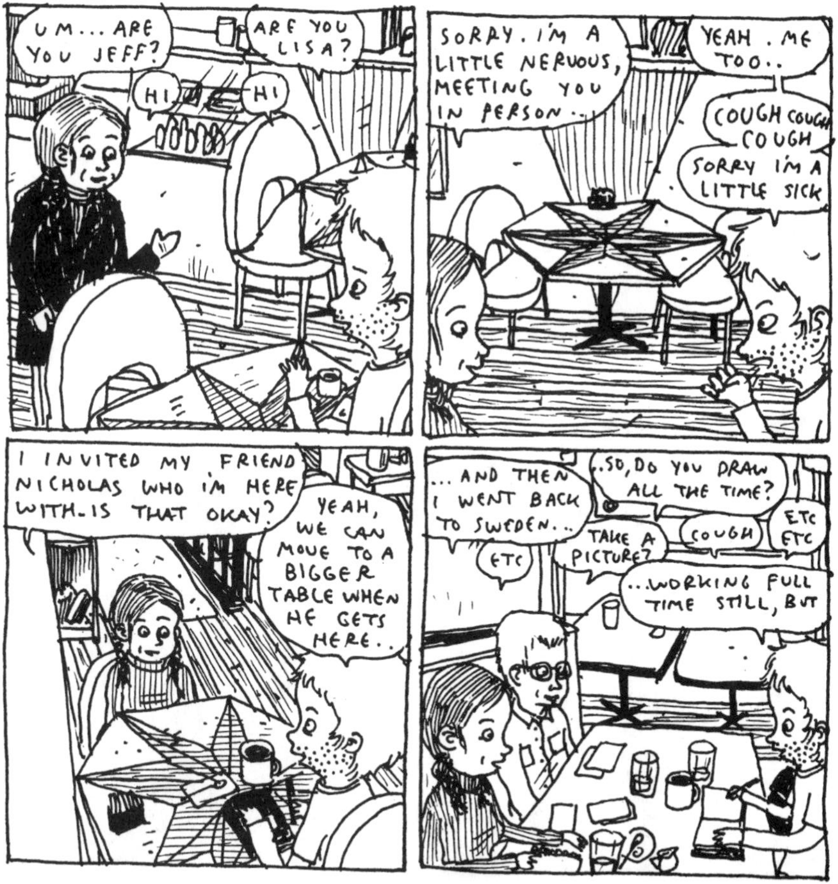
UM... ARE YOU JEFF?
ARE YOU LISA?
HI
HI
SORRY. I'M A LITTLE NERVOUS, MEETING YOU IN PERSON..
YEAH. ME TOO..
COUGH COUGH COUGH
SORRY I'M A LITTLE SICK
I INVITED MY FRIEND NICHOLAS WHO I'M HERE WITH. IS THAT OKAY?
YEAH, WE CAN MOVE TO A BIGGER TABLE WHEN HE GETS HERE..
... AND THEN I WENT BACK TO SWEDEN...
..SO, DO YOU DRAW ALL THE TIME?
ETC
TAKE A PICTURE?
COUGH
ETC ETC
...WORKING FULL TIME STILL, BUT

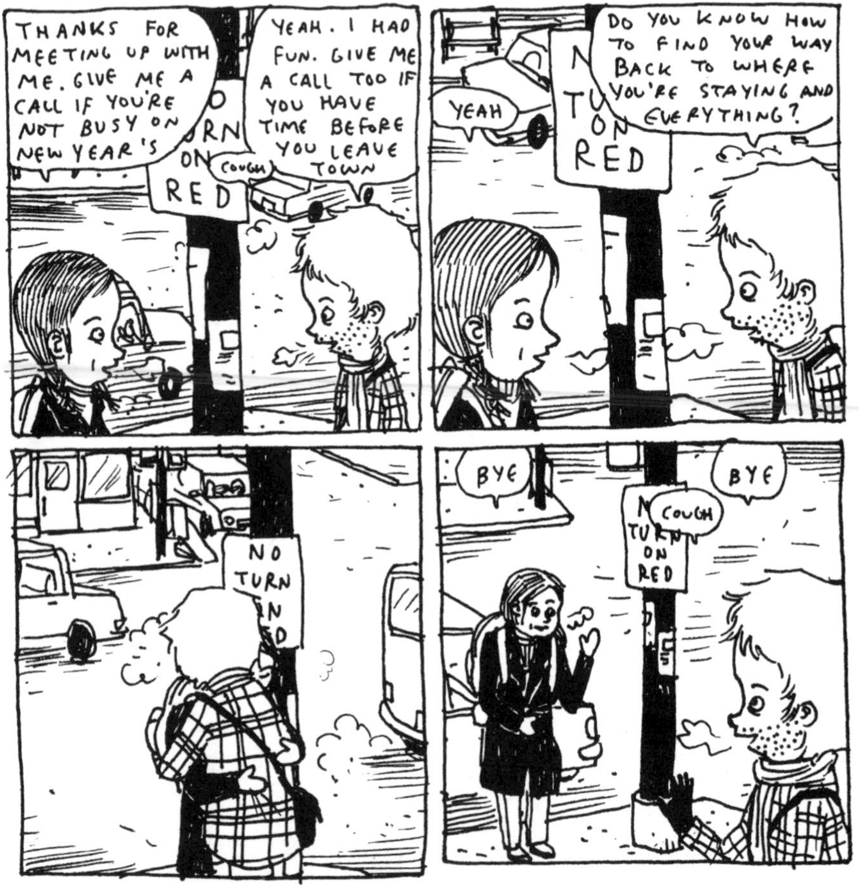
THANKS FOR MEETING UP WITH ME. GIVE ME A CALL IF YOU'RE NOT BUSY ON NEW YEAR'S
YEAH. I HAD FUN. GIVE ME A CALL TOO IF YOU HAVE TIME BEFORE YOU LEAVE TOWN
COUGH
NO TURN ON RED
YEAH
DO YOU KNOW HOW TO FIND YOUR WAY BACK TO WHERE YOU'RE STAYING AND EVERYTHING?
NO TURN ON RED
BYE
BYE
COUGH
NO TURN ON RED

MONDAY

DECEMBER 29

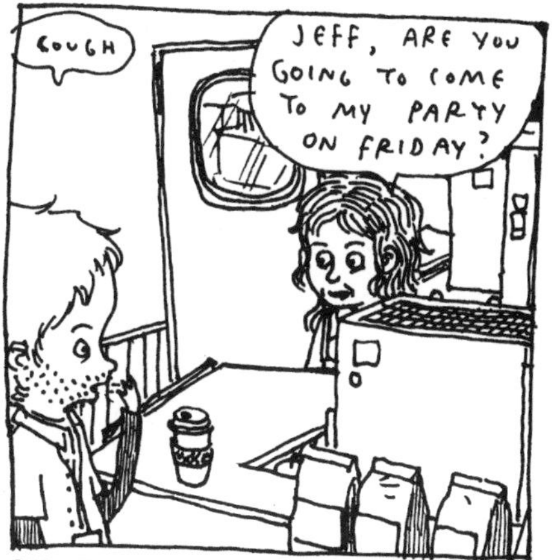
COUGH
JEFF, ARE YOU GOING TO COME TO MY PARTY ON FRIDAY?

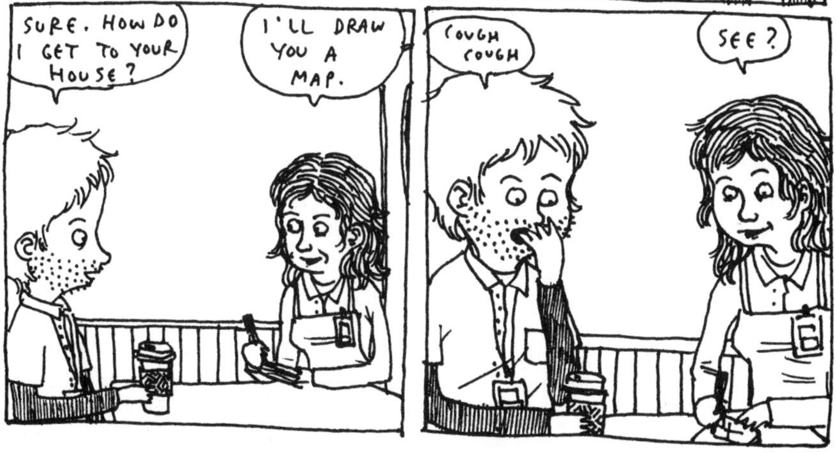
SURE. HOW DO I GET TO YOUR HOUSE?
I'LL DRAW YOU A MAP.
COUGH COUGH
SEE?

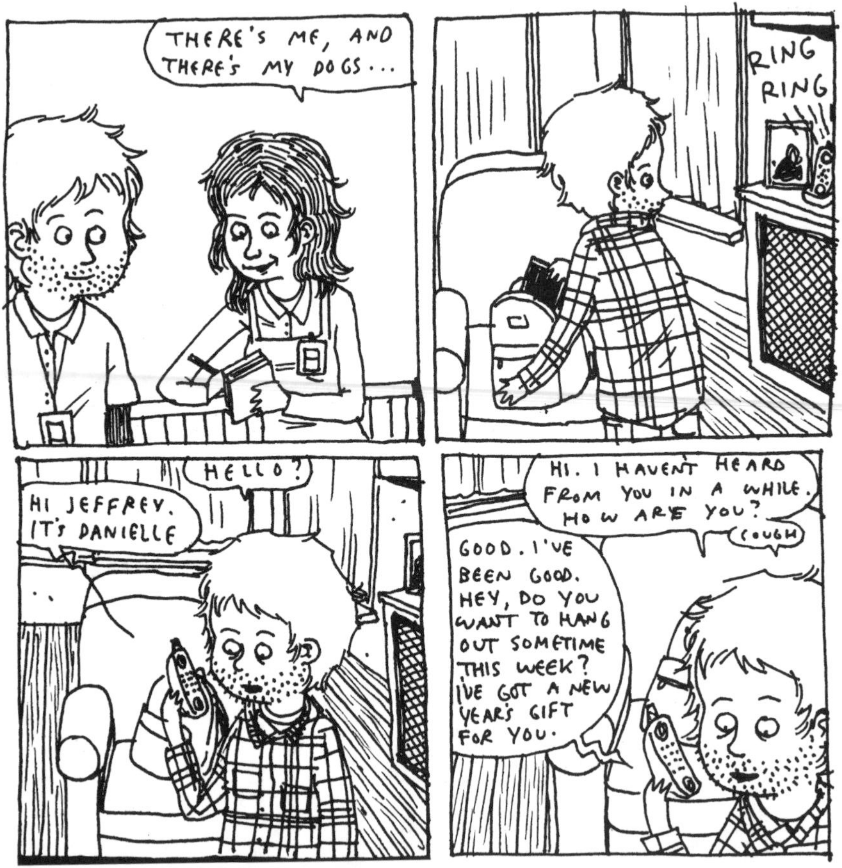
THERE'S ME, AND THERE'S MY DOGS...
RING RING
HELLO?
HI JEFFREY. IT'S DANIELLE
HI. I HAVEN'T HEARD FROM YOU IN A WHILE. HOW ARE YOU?
COUGH
GOOD. I'VE BEEN GOOD. HEY, DO YOU WANT TO HANG OUT SOMETIME THIS WEEK? I'VE GOT A NEW YEAR'S GIFT FOR YOU.

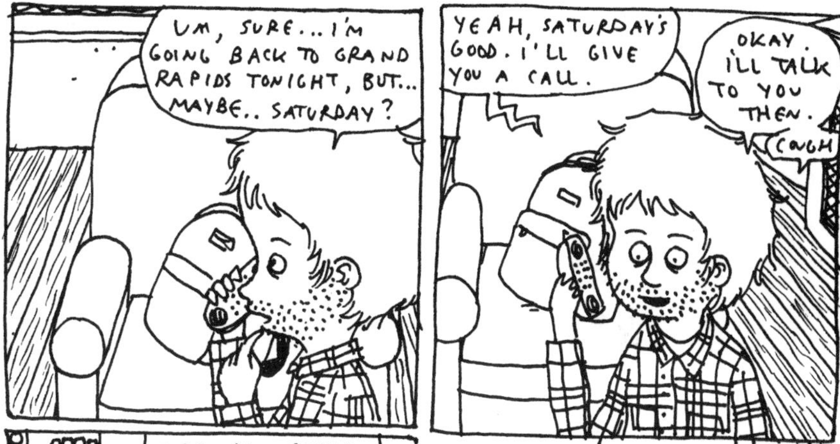
UM, SURE... I'M GOING BACK TO GRAND RAPIDS TONIGHT, BUT... MAYBE.. SATURDAY?
YEAH, SATURDAY'S GOOD. I'LL GIVE YOU A CALL.
OKAY. I'LL TALK TO YOU THEN.
COUGH

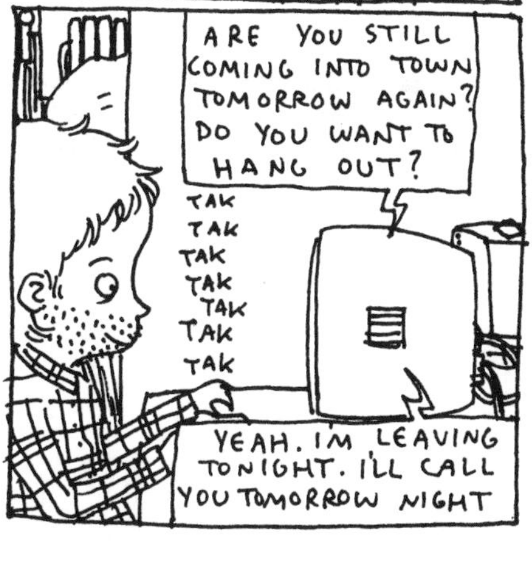
ARE YOU STILL COMING INTO TOWN TOMORROW AGAIN? DO YOU WANT TO HANG OUT?
TAK TAK TAK TAK TAK TAK TAK
YEAH. IM LEAVING TONIGHT. I'LL CALL YOU TOMORROW NIGHT

TUESDAY

DECEMBER 30

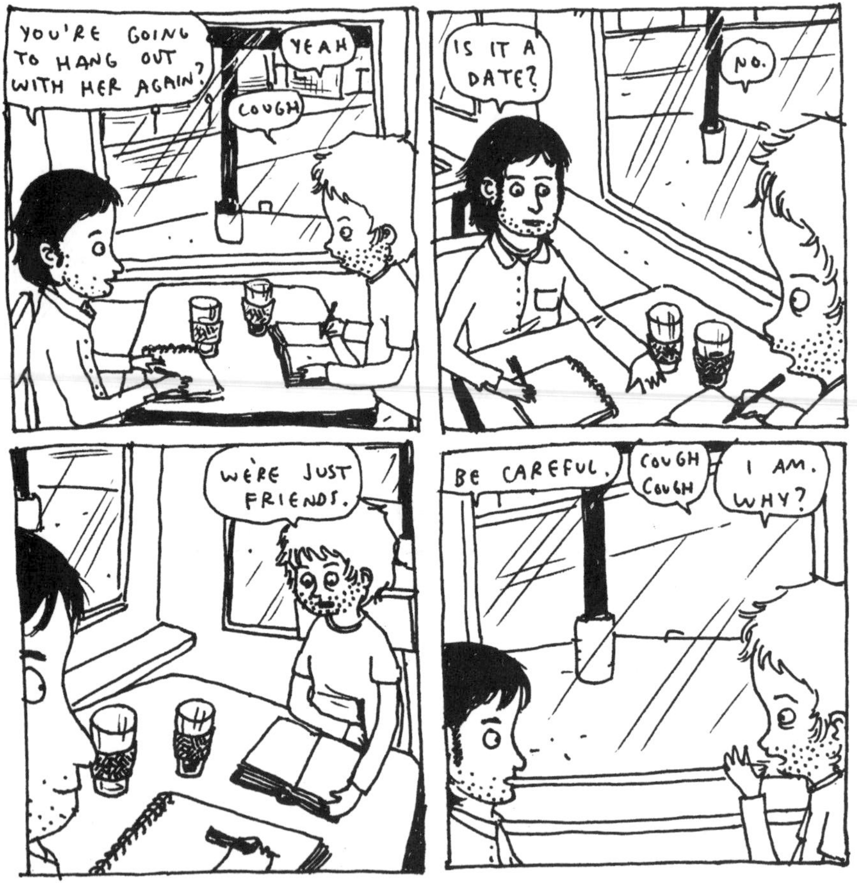
YOU'RE GOING TO HANG OUT WITH HER AGAIN?
YEAH
COUGH
IS IT A DATE?
NO.
WE'RE JUST FRIENDS.
BE CAREFUL.
COUGH COUGH
I AM. WHY?

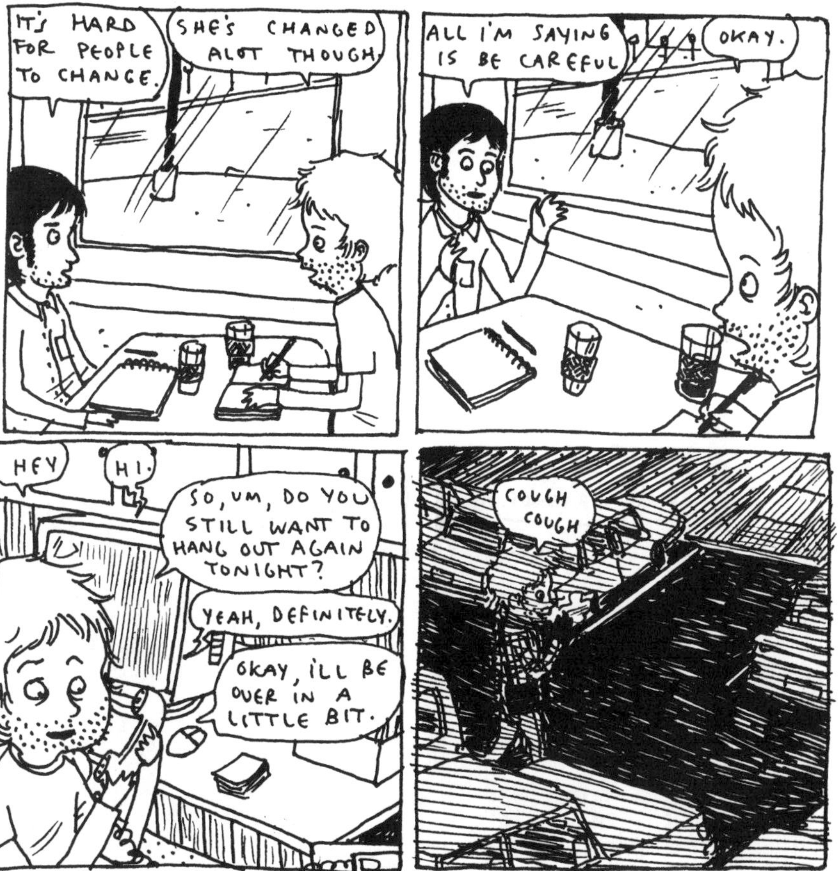
IT'S HARD FOR PEOPLE TO CHANGE.
SHE'S CHANGED ALOT THOUGH.
ALL I'M SAYING IS BE CAREFUL
OKAY.
HEY
HI.
SO, UM, DO YOU STILL WANT TO HANG OUT AGAIN TONIGHT?
YEAH, DEFINITELY.
OKAY, I'LL BE OVER IN A LITTLE BIT.
COUGH COUGH

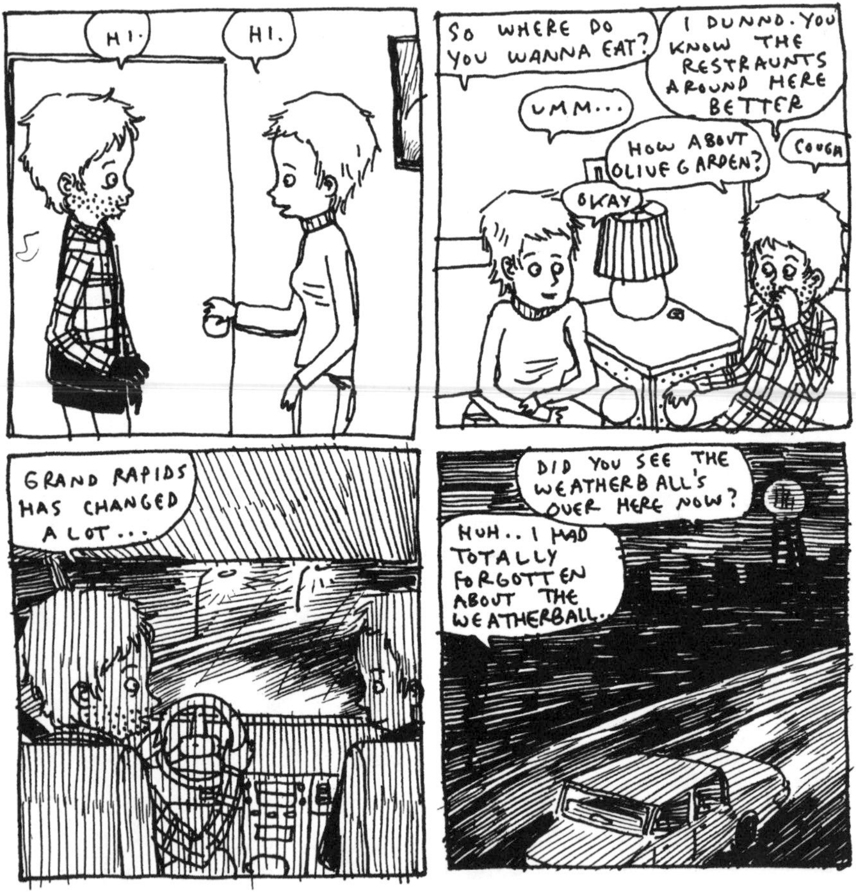
HI.
HI.
SO WHERE DO YOU WANNA EAT?
I DUNNO. YOU KNOW THE RESTRAUNTS AROUND HERE BETTER
UMM...
HOW ABOUT OLIVE GARDEN?
COUGH
OKAY
GRAND RAPIDS HAS CHANGED A LOT...
DID YOU SEE THE WEATHERBALL'S OVER HERE NOW?
HUH.. I HAD TOTALLY FORGOTTEN ABOUT THE WEATHERBALL..

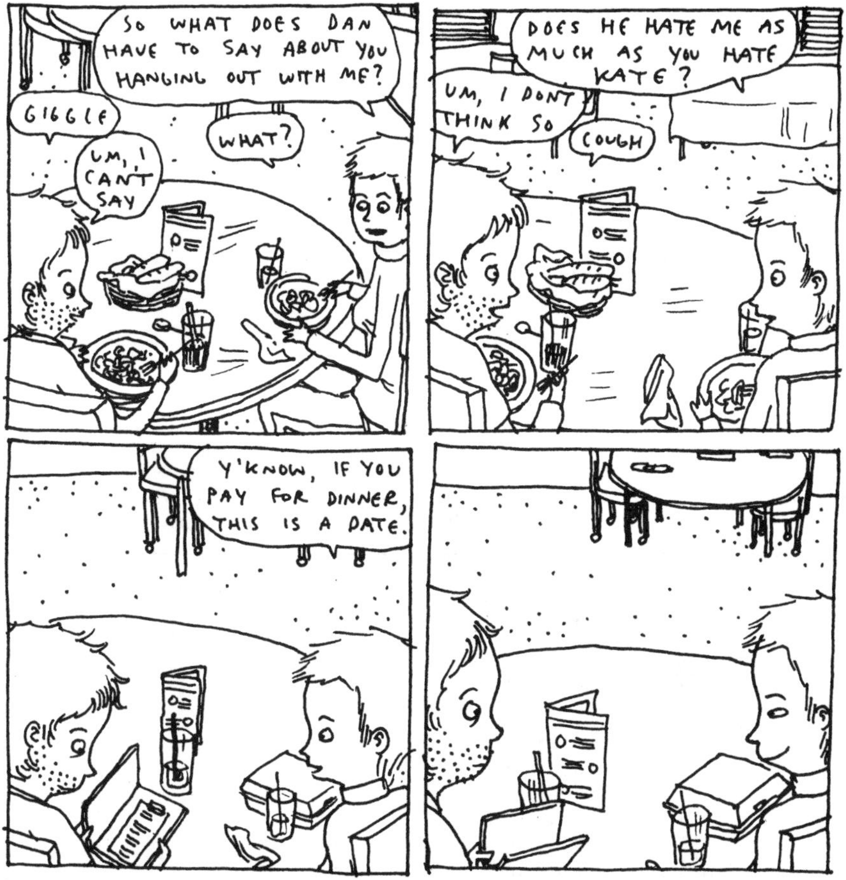
SO WHAT DOES DAN HAVE TO SAY ABOUT YOU HANGING OUT WITH ME?
GIGGLE
WHAT?
UM, I CAN'T SAY
DOES HE HATE ME AS MUCH AS YOU HATE KATE?
UM, I DONT THINK SO
COUGH
Y'KNOW, IF YOU PAY FOR DINNER, THIS IS A DATE.

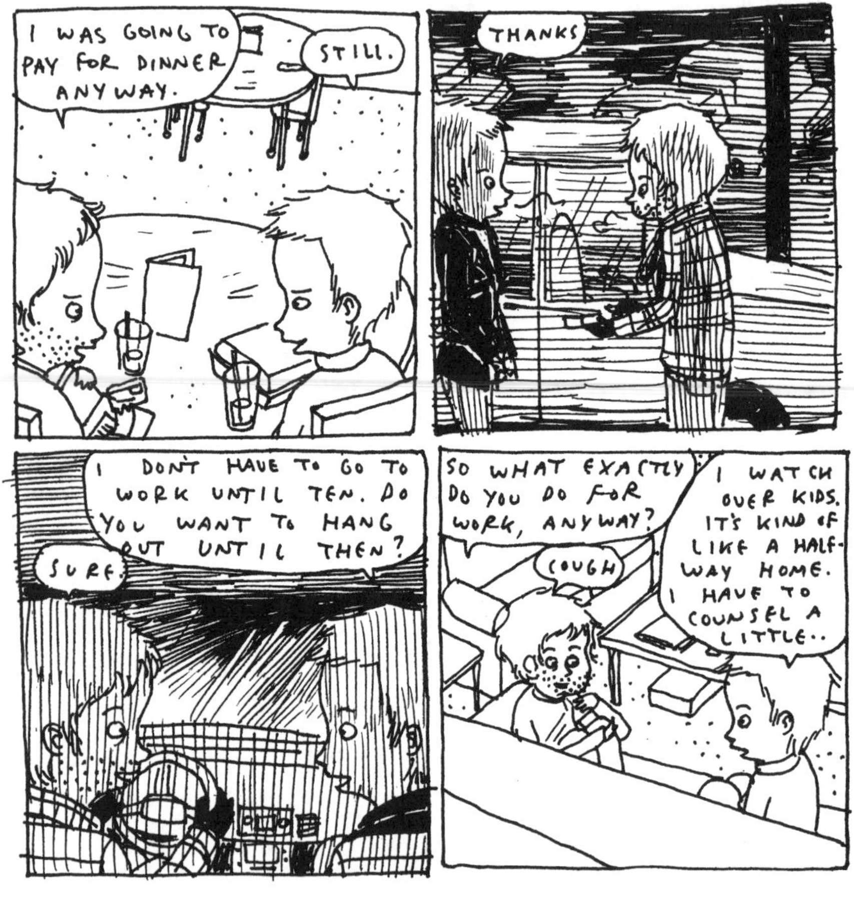
I WAS GOING TO PAY FOR DINNER ANYWAY.
STILL.
THANKS
I DON'T HAVE TO GO TO WORK UNTIL TEN. DO YOU WANT TO HANG OUT UNTIL THEN?
SURE.
SO WHAT EXACTLY DO YOU DO FOR WORK, ANYWAY?
COUGH
I WATCH OVER KIDS. IT'S KIND OF LIKE A HALF-WAY HOME. I HAVE TO COUNSEL A LITTLE..

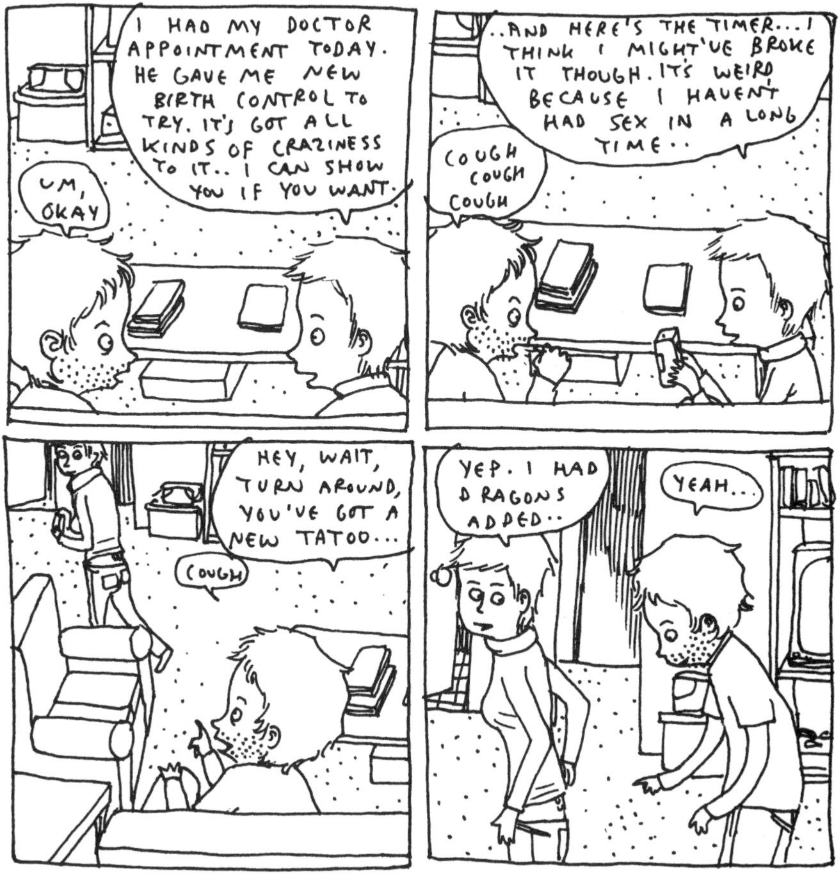
I HAD MY DOCTOR APPOINTMENT TODAY. HE GAVE ME NEW BIRTH CONTROL TO TRY. IT'S GOT ALL KINDS OF CRAZINESS TO IT.. I CAN SHOW YOU IF YOU WANT.
UM, OKAY
..AND HERE'S THE TIMER...I THINK I MIGHT'VE BROKE IT THOUGH. IT'S WEIRD BECAUSE I HAVEN'T HAD SEX IN A LONG TIME..
COUGH COUGH COUGH
HEY, WAIT, TURN AROUND, YOU'VE GOT A NEW TATOO...
COUGH
YEP. I HAD DRAGONS ADDED..
YEAH...

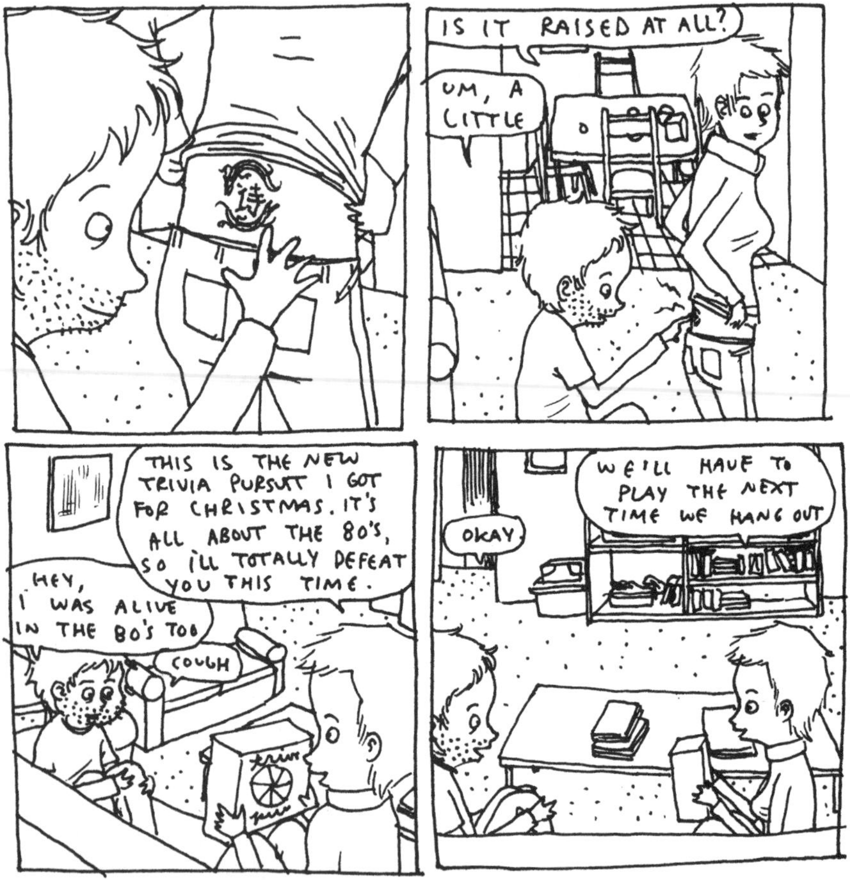
IS IT RAISED AT ALL?
UM, A LITTLE
THIS IS THE NEW TRIVIA PURSUIT I GOT FOR CHRISTMAS. IT'S ALL ABOUT THE 80'S, SO I'LL TOTALLY DEFEAT YOU THIS TIME.
HEY, I WAS ALIVE IN THE 80'S TOO
COUGH
WE'LL HAVE TO PLAY THE NEXT TIME WE HANG OUT
OKAY

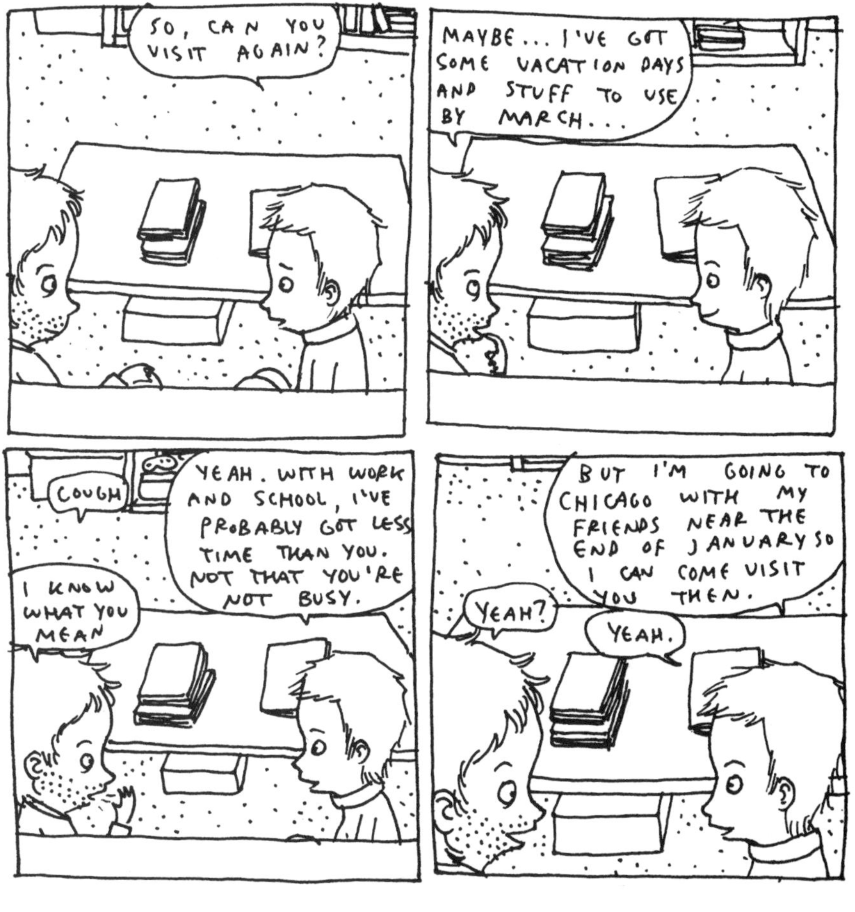
SO, CAN YOU VISIT AGAIN?
MAYBE... I'VE GOT SOME VACATION DAYS AND STUFF TO USE BY MARCH...
COUGH
YEAH. WITH WORK AND SCHOOL, I'VE PROBABLY GOT LESS TIME THAN YOU. NOT THAT YOU'RE NOT BUSY.
I KNOW WHAT YOU MEAN
BUT I'M GOING TO CHICAGO WITH MY FRIENDS NEAR THE END OF JANUARY SO I CAN COME VISIT YOU THEN.
YEAH?
YEAH.

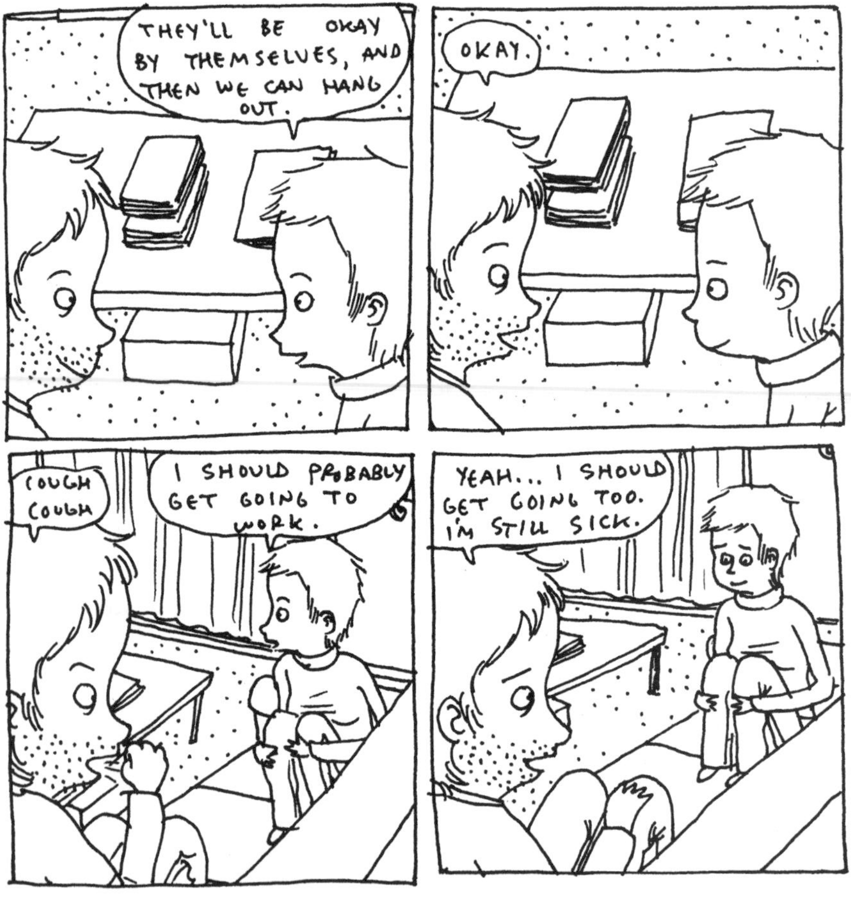
THEY'LL BE OKAY BY THEMSELVES, AND THEN WE CAN HANG OUT.
OKAY.
COUGH COUGH
I SHOULD PROBABLY GET GOING TO WORK.
YEAH... I SHOULD GET GOING TOO. I'M STILL SICK.

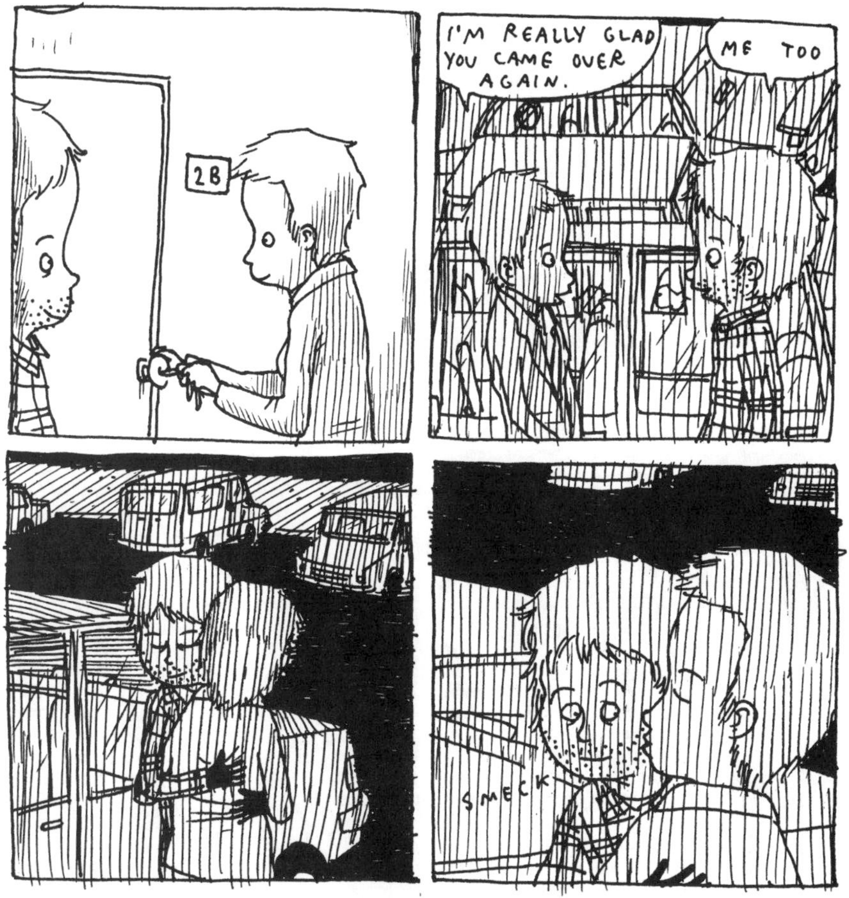
2B
I'M REALLY GLAD YOU CAME OVER AGAIN.
ME TOO
SMECK

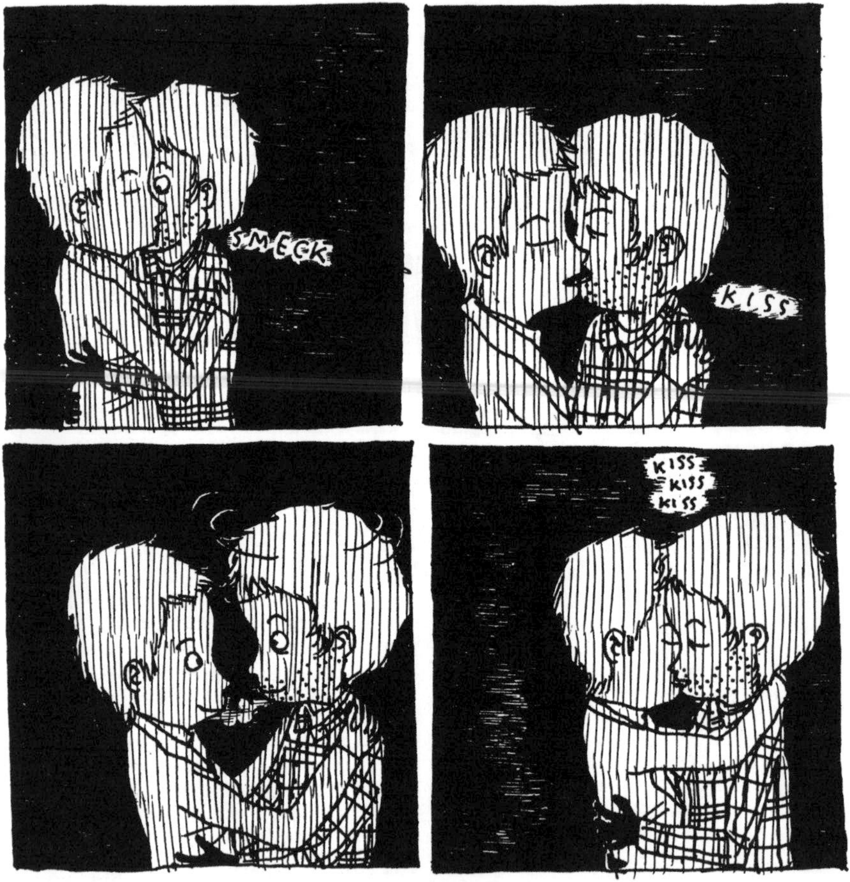
SMECK
KISS
KISS
KISS
KISS

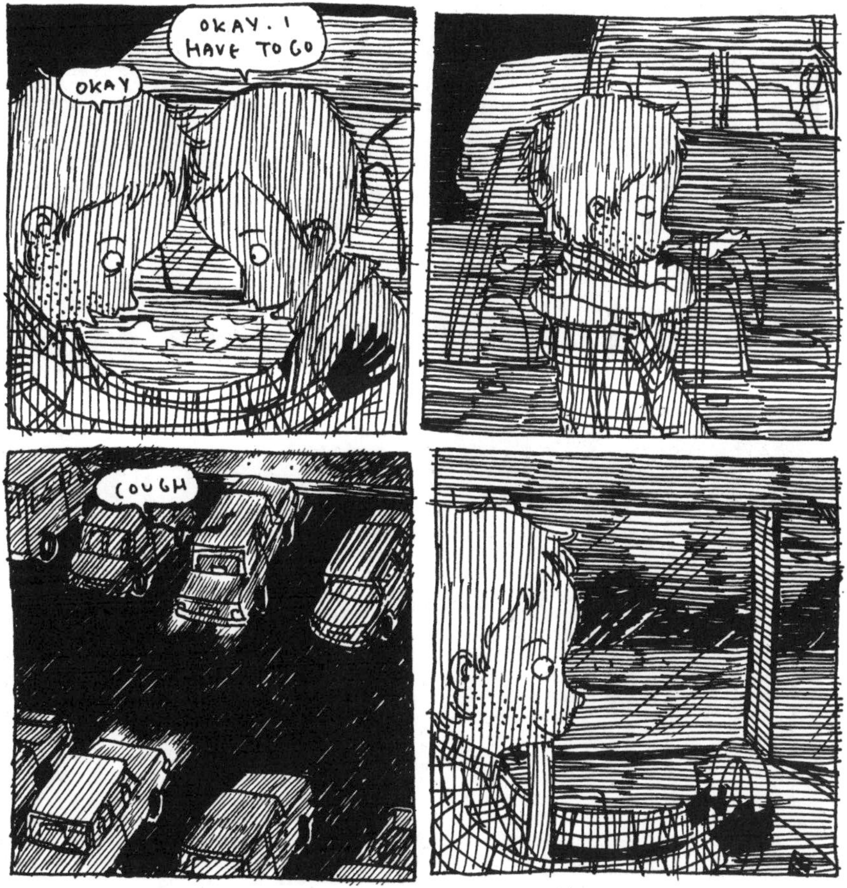
OKAY. I HAVE TO GO
OKAY
COUGH

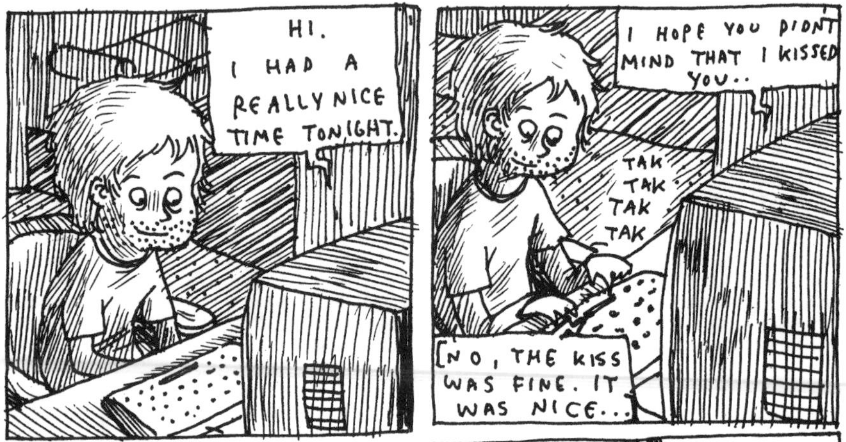
HI.
I HAD A REALLY NICE TIME TONIGHT.
I HOPE YOU DIDN'T MIND THAT I KISSED YOU..
TAK TAK TAK TAK
NO, THE KISS WAS FINE. IT WAS NICE...

WEDNESDAY

DECEMBER 31

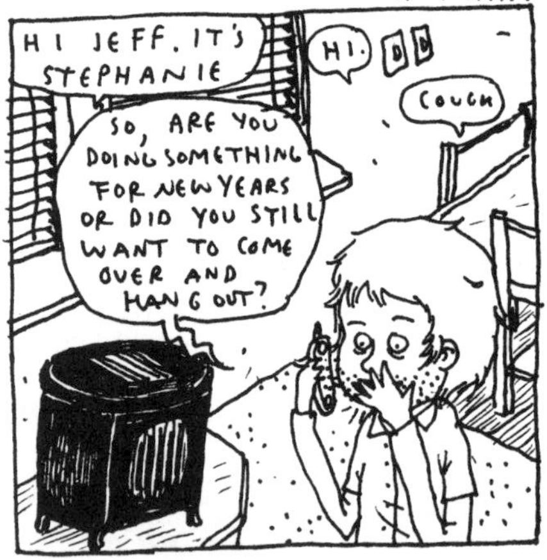
HI JEFF. IT'S STEPHANIE
HI.
COUGH
SO, ARE YOU DOING SOMETHING FOR NEW YEARS OR DID YOU STILL WANT TO COME OVER AND HANG OUT?

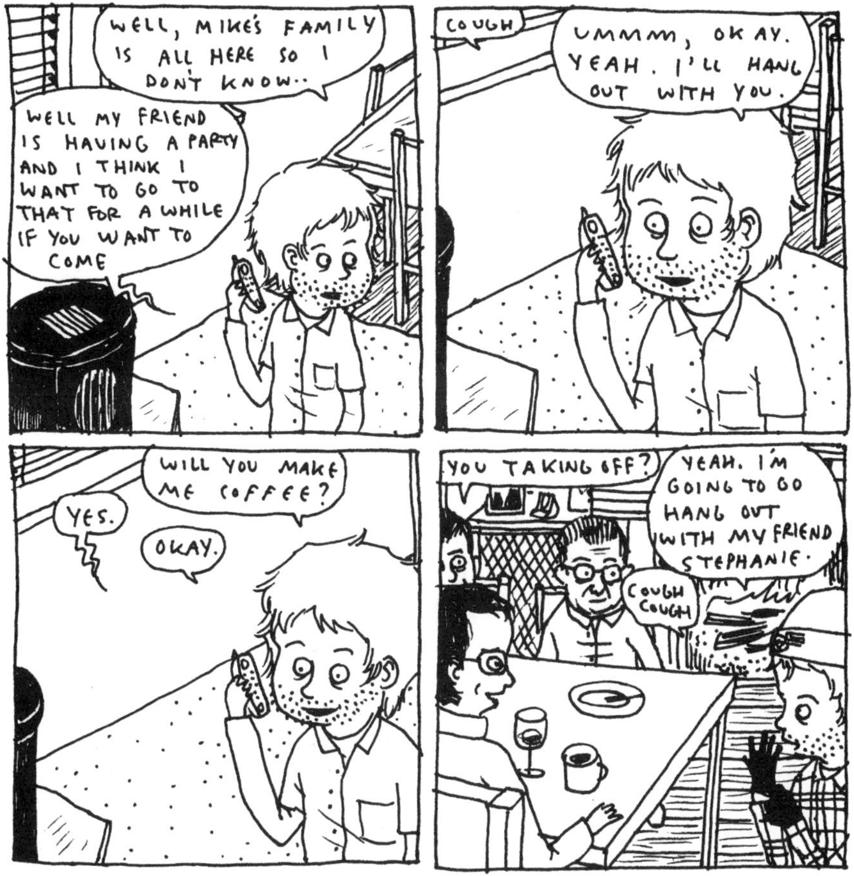
WELL, MIKE'S FAMILY IS ALL HERE SO I DON'T KNOW..
WELL MY FRIEND IS HAVING A PARTY AND I THINK I WANT TO GO TO THAT FOR A WHILE IF YOU WANT TO COME
COUGH
UMMMM, OKAY. YEAH. I'LL HANG OUT WITH YOU.
WILL YOU MAKE ME COFFEE?
YES.
OKAY.
YOU TAKING OFF?
YEAH. I'M GOING TO GO HANG OUT WITH MY FRIEND STEPHANIE.
COUGH COUGH

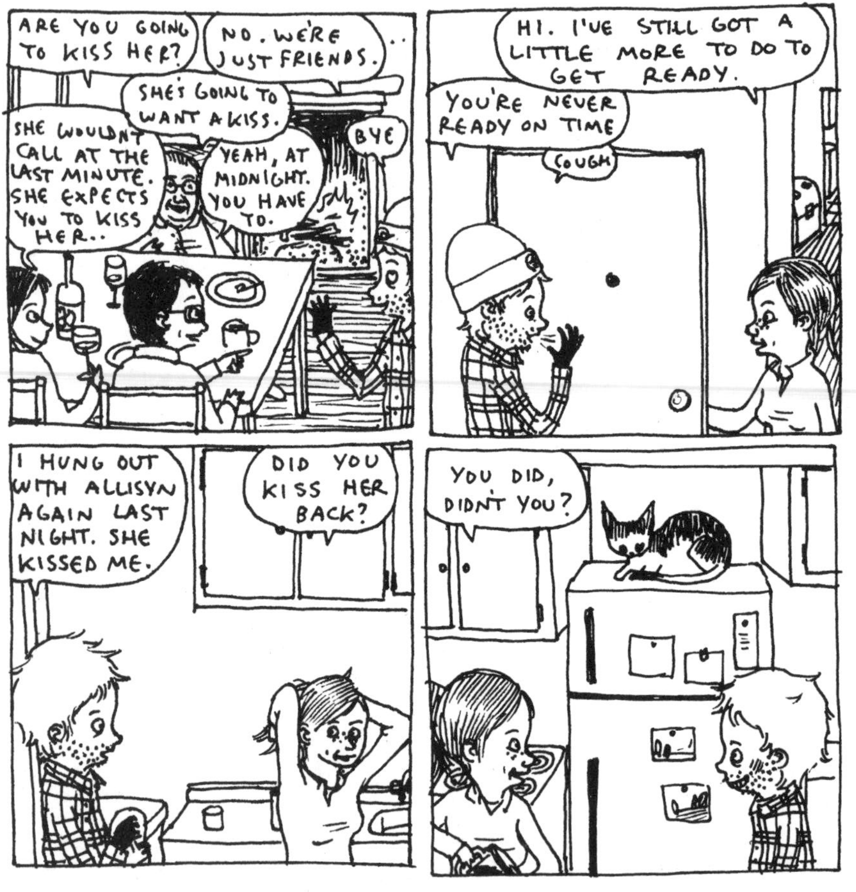
ARE YOU GOING TO KISS HER?
NO. WE'RE JUST FRIENDS. . .
SHE'S GOING TO WANT A KISS.
SHE WOULDN'T CALL AT THE LAST MINUTE. SHE EXPECTS YOU TO KISS HER..
YEAH, AT MIDNIGHT. YOU HAVE TO.
BYE
HI. I'VE STILL GOT A LITTLE MORE TO DO TO GET READY.
YOU'RE NEVER READY ON TIME
COUGH
I HUNG OUT WITH ALLISYN AGAIN LAST NIGHT. SHE KISSED ME.
DID YOU KISS HER BACK?
YOU DID, DIDN'T YOU?

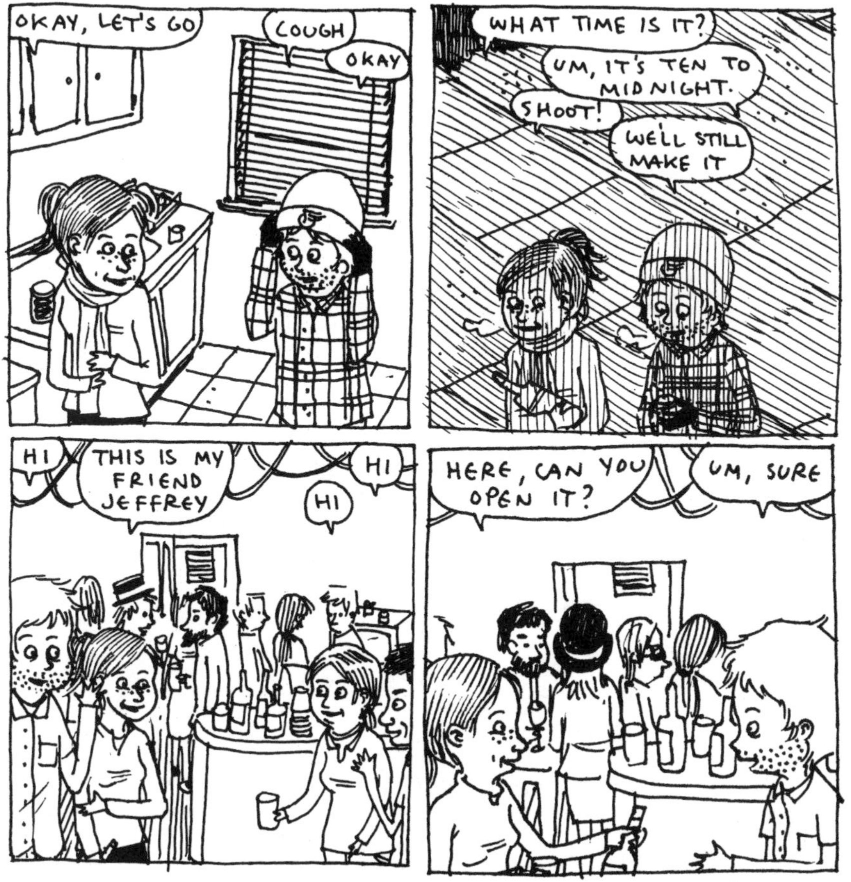
OKAY, LET'S GO
COUGH
OKAY
WHAT TIME IS IT?
UM, IT'S TEN TO MIDNIGHT.
SHOOT!
WE'LL STILL MAKE IT
HI
THIS IS MY FRIEND JEFFREY
HI
HI
HERE, CAN YOU OPEN IT?
UM, SURE

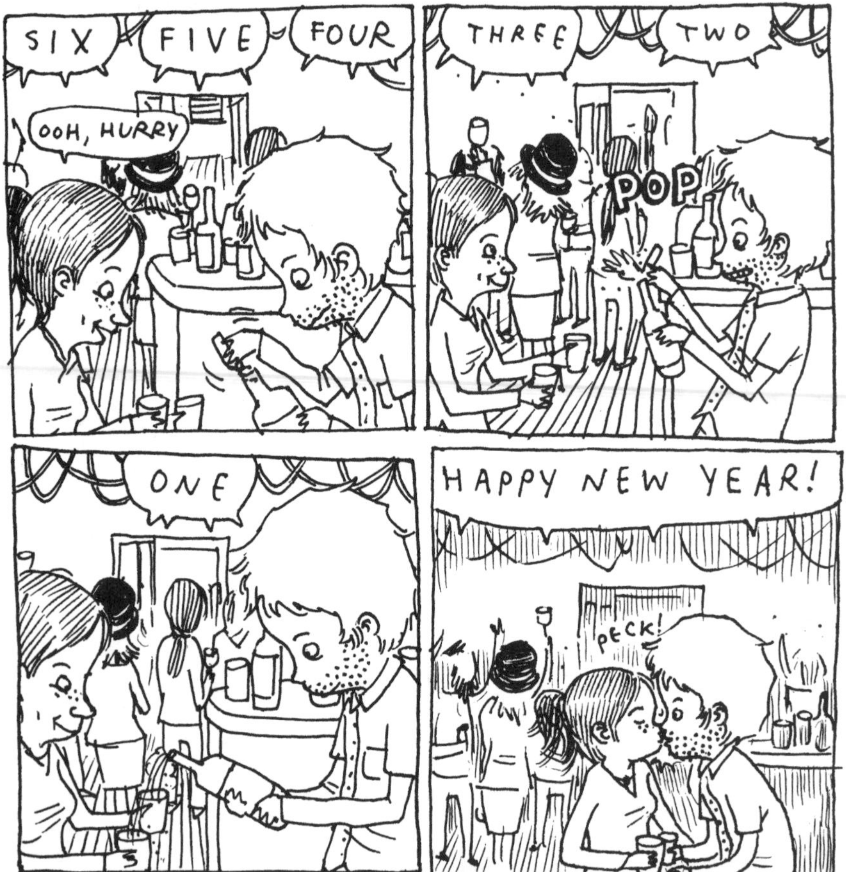
SIX
FIVE
FOUR
OOH, HURRY
THREE
TWO
POP
ONE
HAPPY NEW YEAR!
PECK!

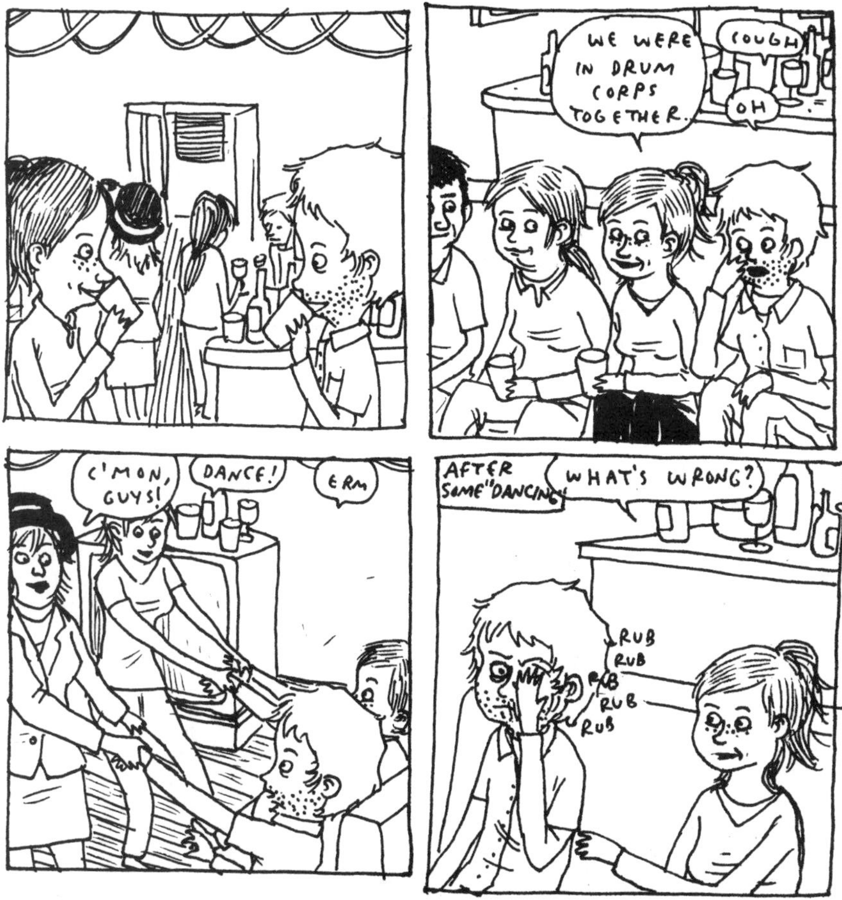
WE WERE IN DRUM CORPS TOGETHER.
COUGH
OH
C'MON, GUYS!
DANCE!
ERM
AFTER SOME "DANCING"
WHAT'S WRONG?
RUB
RUB
RUB
RUB
RUB

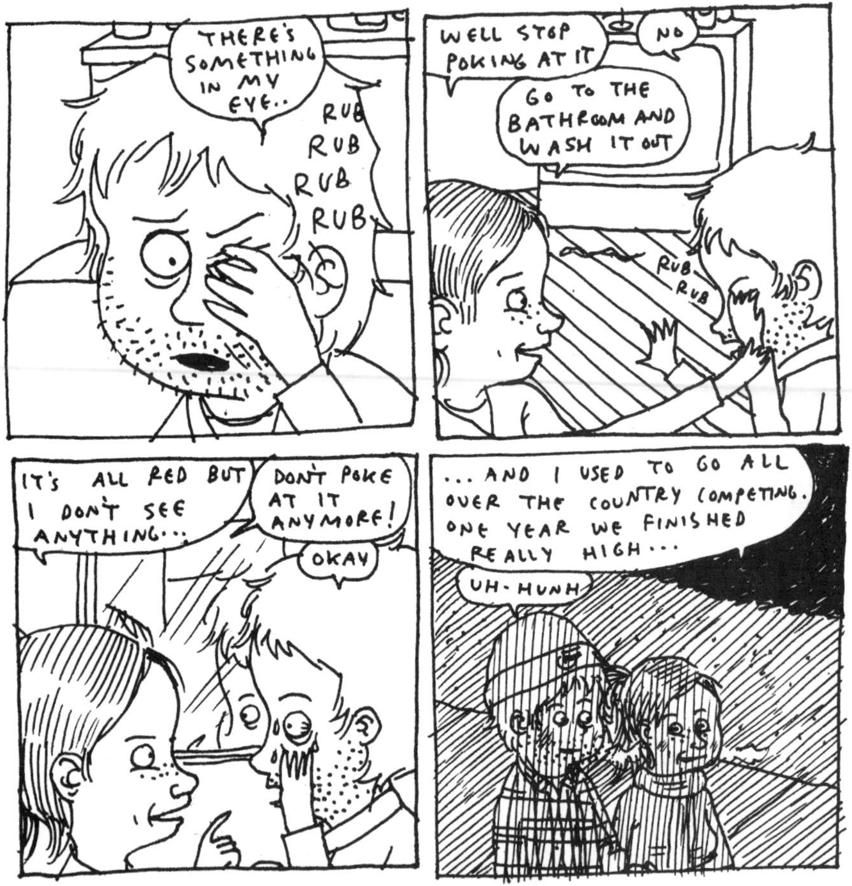
THERE'S SOMETHING IN MY EYE..
RUB RUB RUB RUB
WELL STOP POKING AT IT
NO
GO TO THE BATHROOM AND WASH IT OUT
RUB RUB
IT'S ALL RED BUT I DON'T SEE ANYTHING...
DON'T POKE AT IT ANYMORE!
OKAY
...AND I USED TO GO ALL OVER THE COUNTRY COMPETING. ONE YEAR WE FINISHED REALLY HIGH...
UH-HUNH

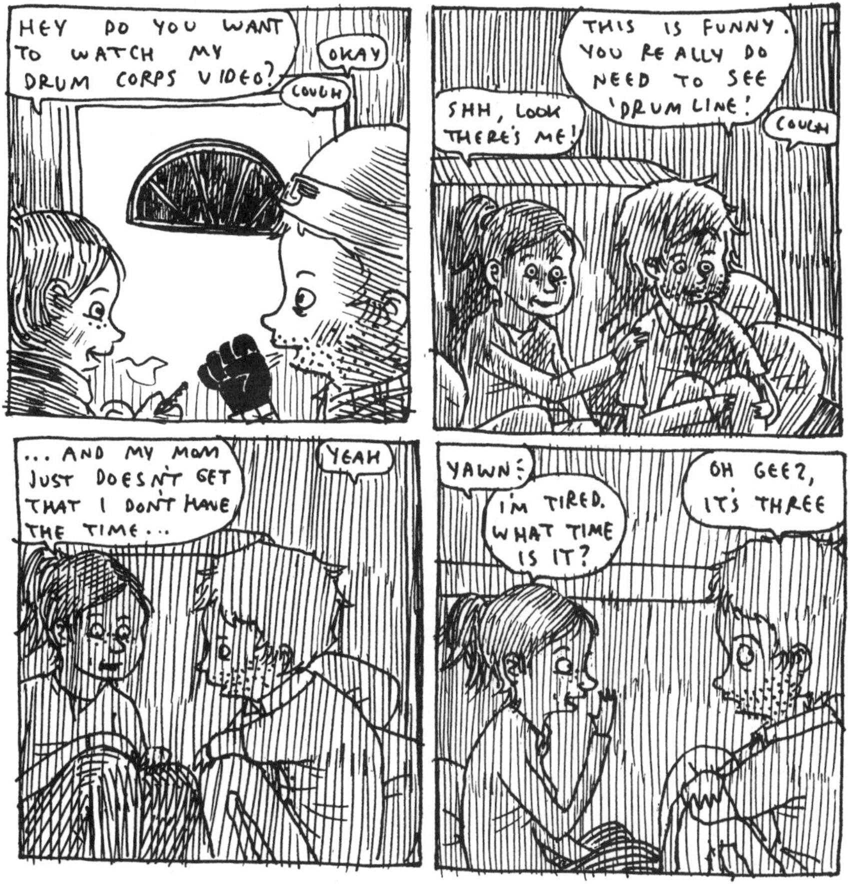
HEY DO YOU WANT TO WATCH MY DRUM CORPS VIDEO?
OKAY
COUGH
THIS IS FUNNY. YOU REALLY DO NEED TO SEE 'DRUM LINE'
SHH, LOOK THERE'S ME!
COUGH
... AND MY MOM JUST DOESN'T GET THAT I DON'T HAVE THE TIME...
YEAH
YAWN
I'M TIRED. WHAT TIME IS IT?
OH GEEZ, IT'S THREE

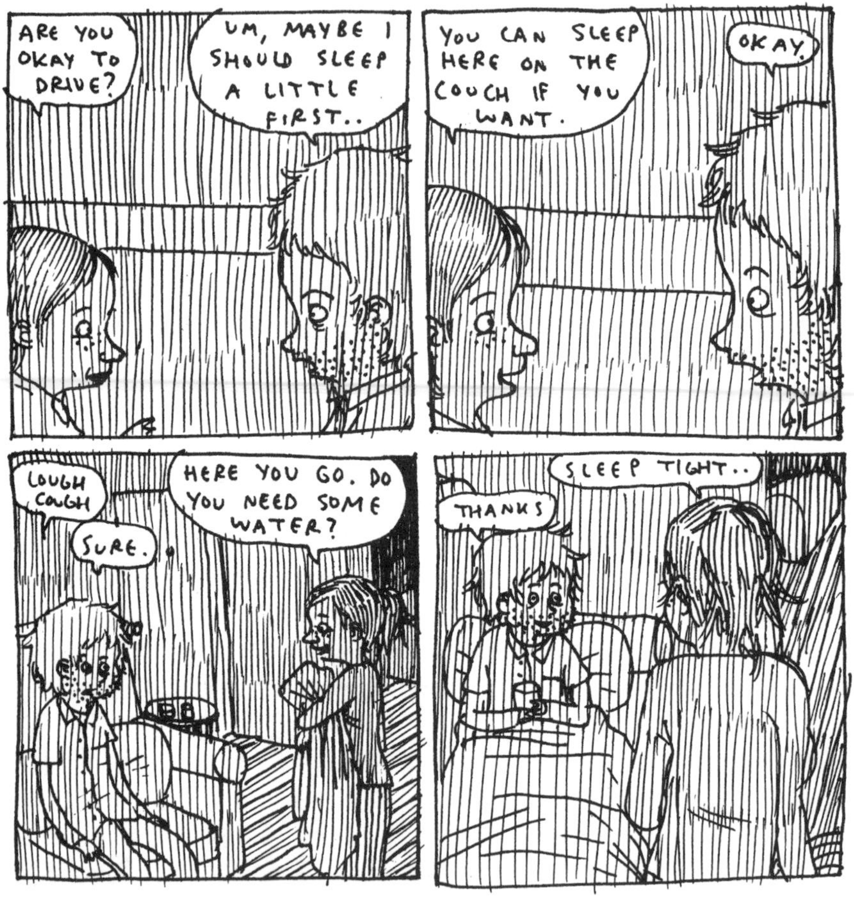
ARE YOU OKAY TO DRIVE?
UM, MAYBE I SHOULD SLEEP A LITTLE FIRST..
YOU CAN SLEEP HERE ON THE COUCH IF YOU WANT.
OKAY.
COUGH COUGH
HERE YOU GO. DO YOU NEED SOME WATER?
SURE.
SLEEP TIGHT..
THANKS

THURSDAY

JANUARY 1

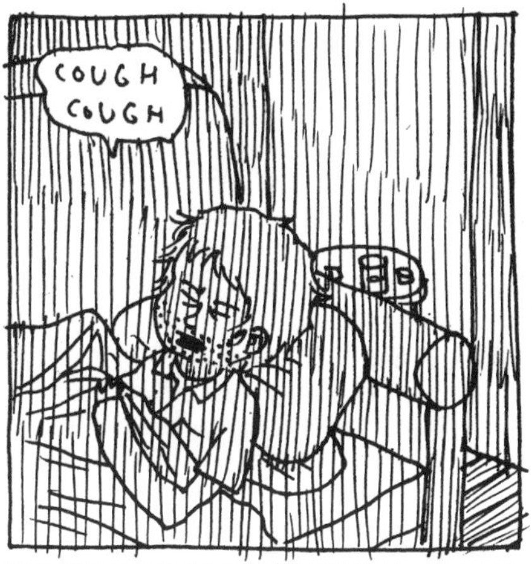
COUGH COUGH

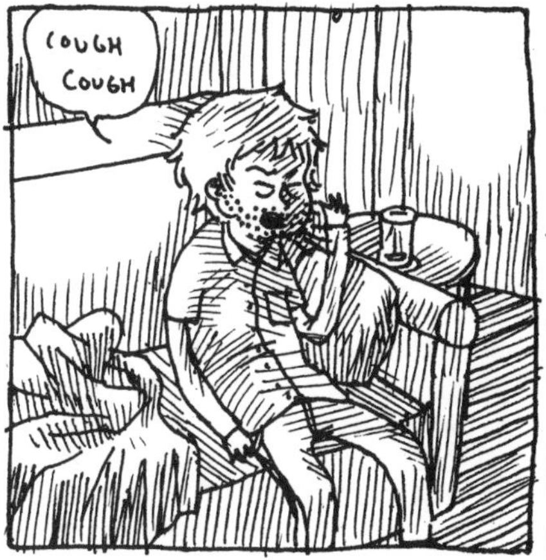
COUGH COUGH

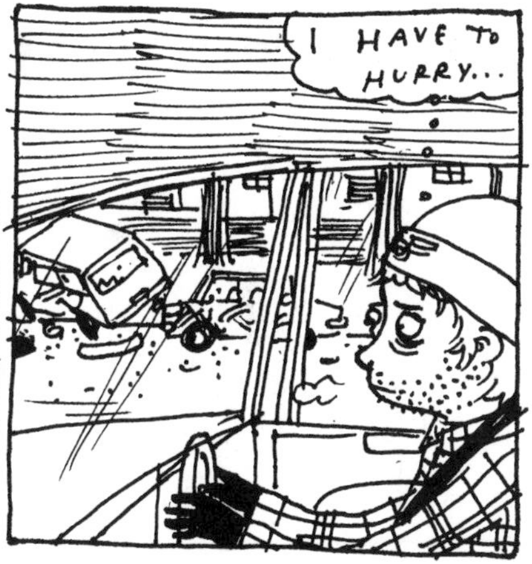
I HAVE TO HURRY...

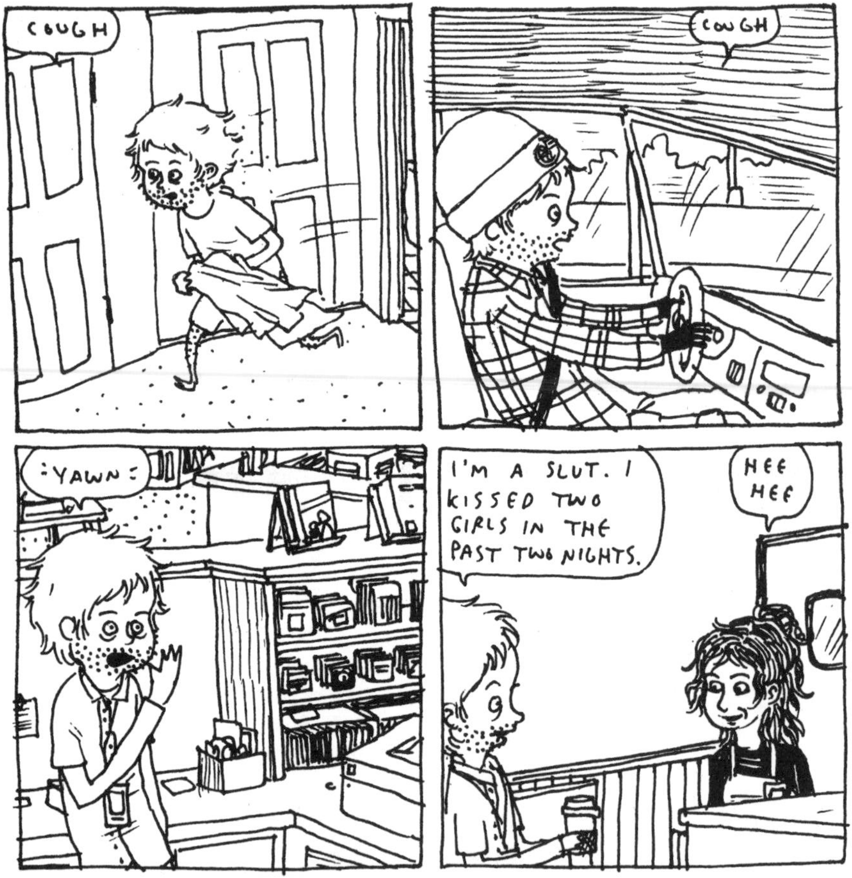
COUGH
COUGH
YAWN
I'M A SLUT. I KISSED TWO GIRLS IN THE PAST TWO NIGHTS.
HEE HEE

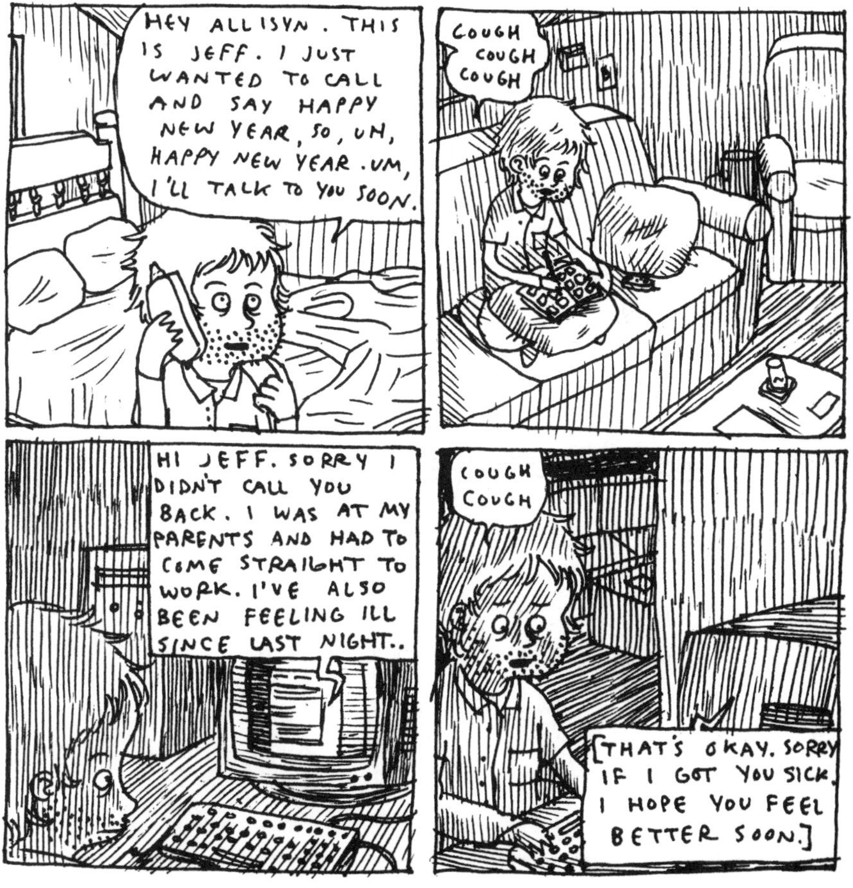
HEY ALLISYN. THIS IS JEFF. I JUST WANTED TO CALL AND SAY HAPPY NEW YEAR, SO, UH, HAPPY NEW YEAR. UM, I'LL TALK TO YOU SOON.
COUGH COUGH COUGH
HI JEFF. SORRY I DIDN'T CALL YOU BACK. I WAS AT MY PARENTS AND HAD TO COME STRAIGHT TO WORK. I'VE ALSO BEEN FEELING ILL SINCE LAST NIGHT..
COUGH COUGH
[THAT'S OKAY. SORRY IF I GOT YOU SICK. I HOPE YOU FEEL BETTER SOON.]

FRIDAY

JANUARY 2

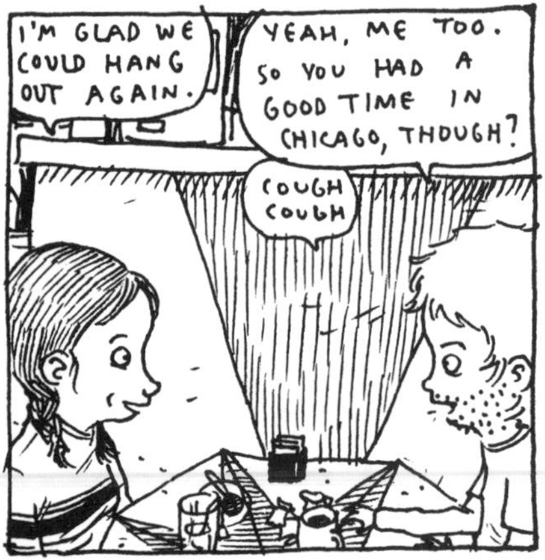
I'M GLAD WE COULD HANG OUT AGAIN.
YEAH, ME TOO. SO YOU HAD A GOOD TIME IN CHICAGO, THOUGH?
COUGH COUGH

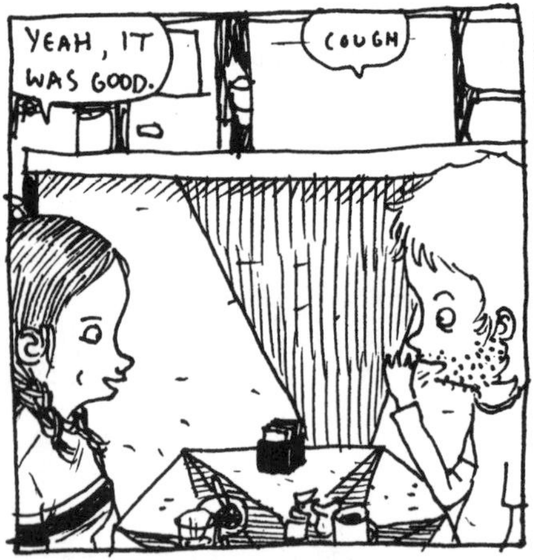
YEAH, IT WAS GOOD.
COUGH

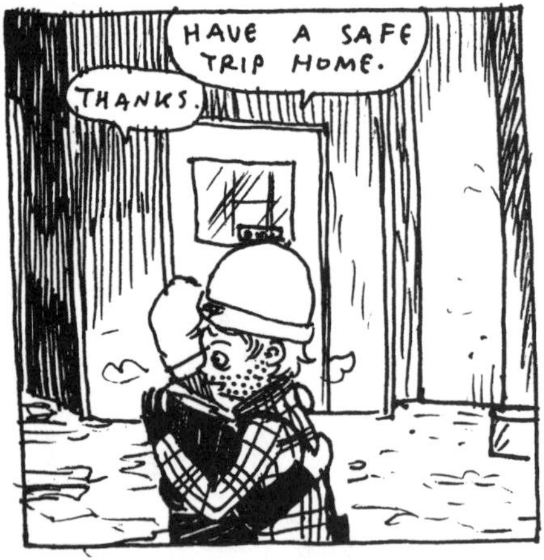
HAVE A SAFE TRIP HOME.
THANKS.

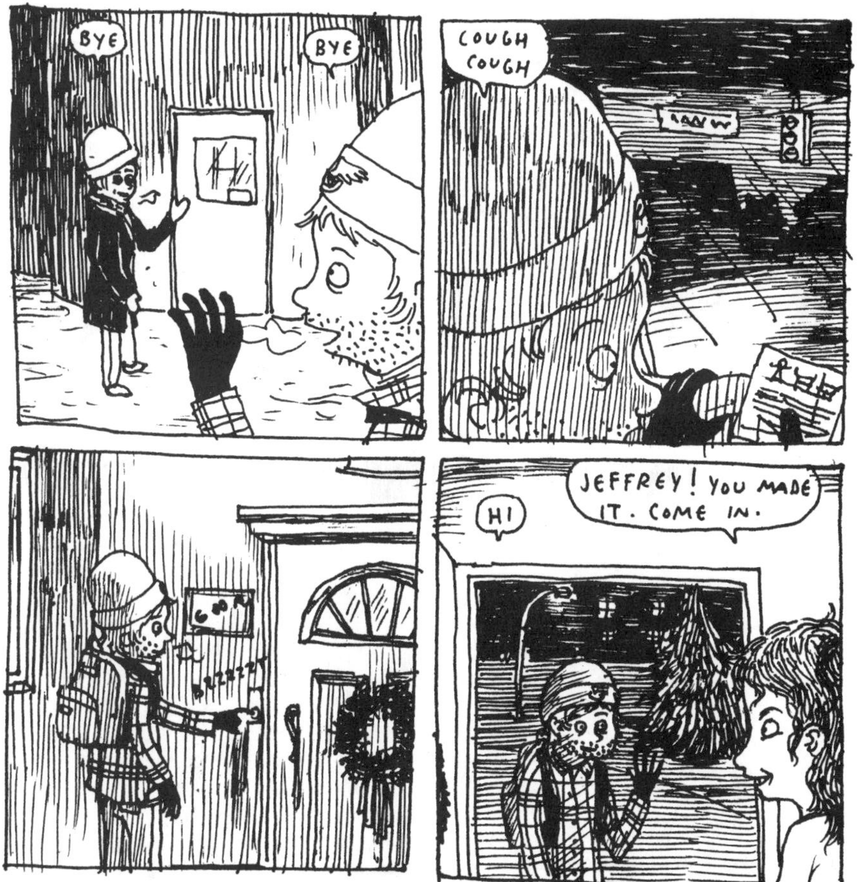
BYE
BYE
COUGH COUGH
HI
JEFFREY! YOU MADE IT. COME IN.

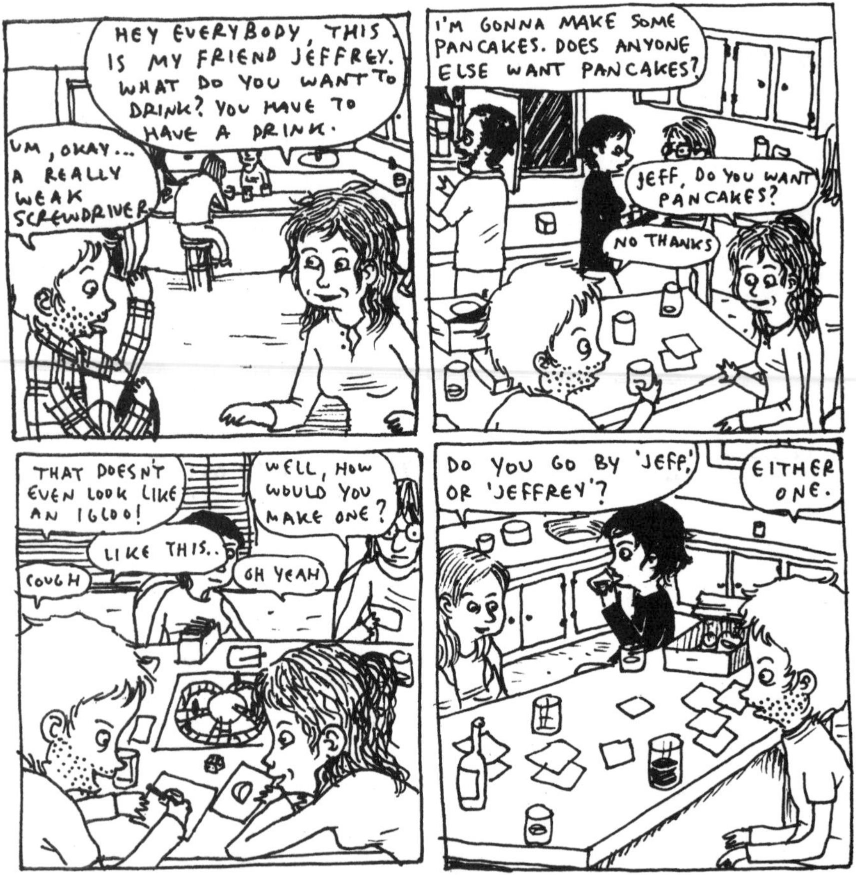
HEY EVERYBODY, THIS IS MY FRIEND JEFFREY. WHAT DO YOU WANT TO DRINK? YOU HAVE TO HAVE A DRINK.
UM, OKAY... A REALLY WEAK SCREWDRIVER
I'M GONNA MAKE SOME PANCAKES. DOES ANYONE ELSE WANT PANCAKES?
JEFF, DO YOU WANT PANCAKES?
NO THANKS
THAT DOESN'T EVEN LOOK LIKE AN IGLOO!
WELL, HOW WOULD YOU MAKE ONE?
LIKE THIS..
COUGH
OH YEAH
DO YOU GO BY 'JEFF,' OR 'JEFFREY'?
EITHER ONE.

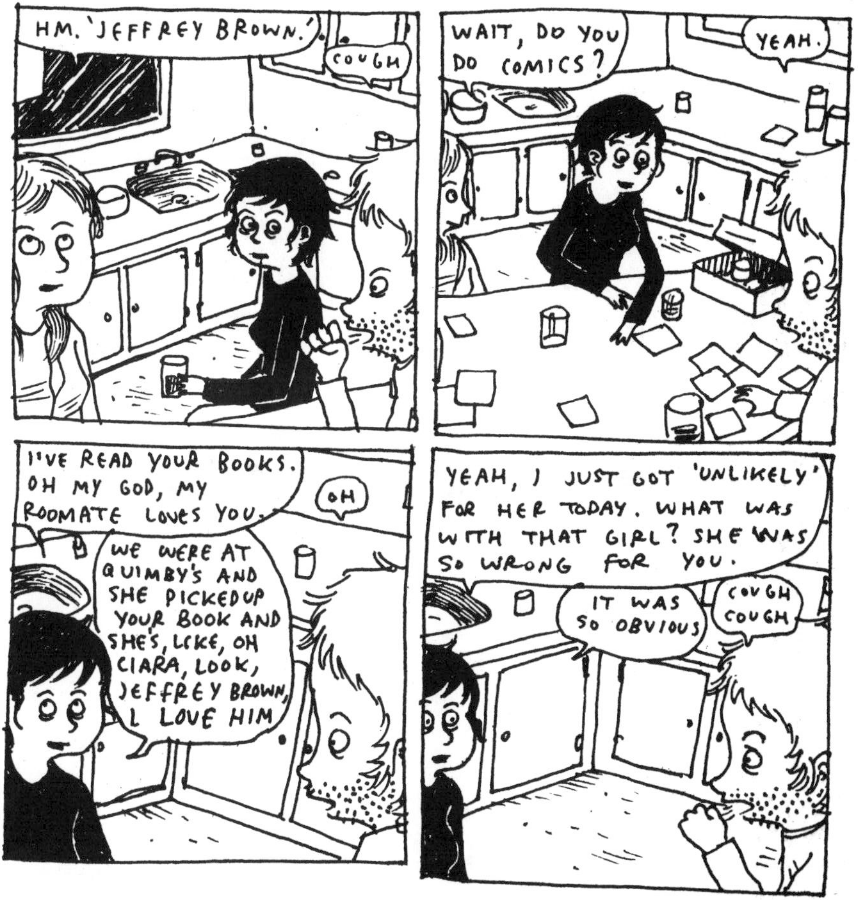
HM. 'JEFFREY BROWN.'
COUGH
WAIT, DO YOU DO COMICS?
YEAH.
I'VE READ YOUR BOOKS. OH MY GOD, MY ROOMATE LOVES YOU.
OH
WE WERE AT QUIMBY'S AND SHE PICKEDUP YOUR BOOK AND SHE'S, LIKE, OH CIARA, LOOK, JEFFREY BROWN, I LOVE HIM
YEAH, I JUST GOT 'UNLIKELY' FOR HER TODAY. WHAT WAS WITH THAT GIRL? SHE WAS SO WRONG FOR YOU.
IT WAS SO OBVIOUS
COUGH COUGH

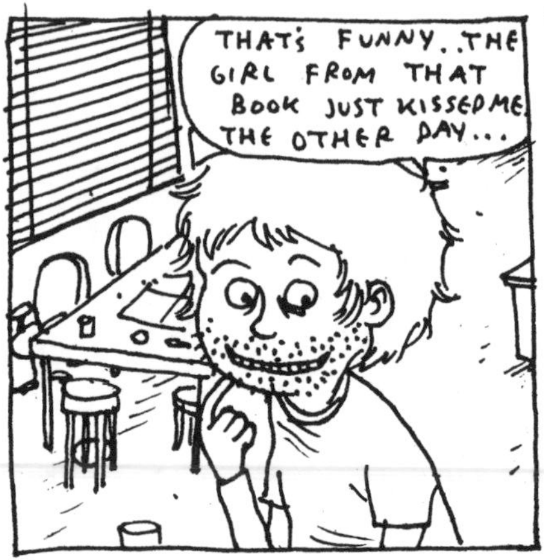
THAT'S FUNNY.. THE GIRL FROM THAT BOOK JUST KISSED ME THE OTHER DAY...

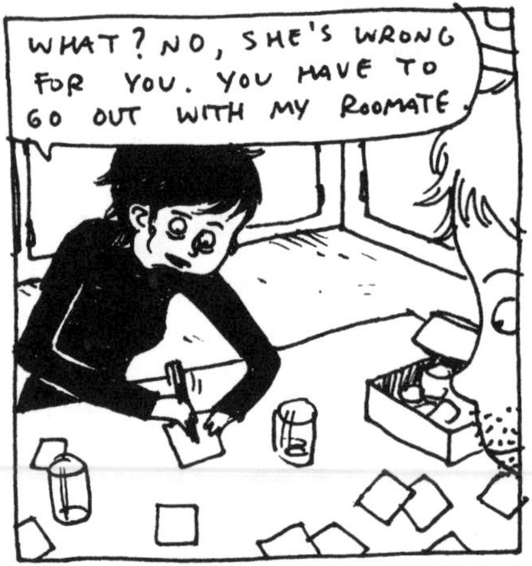
WHAT? NO, SHE'S WRONG FOR YOU. YOU HAVE TO GO OUT WITH MY ROOMATE.

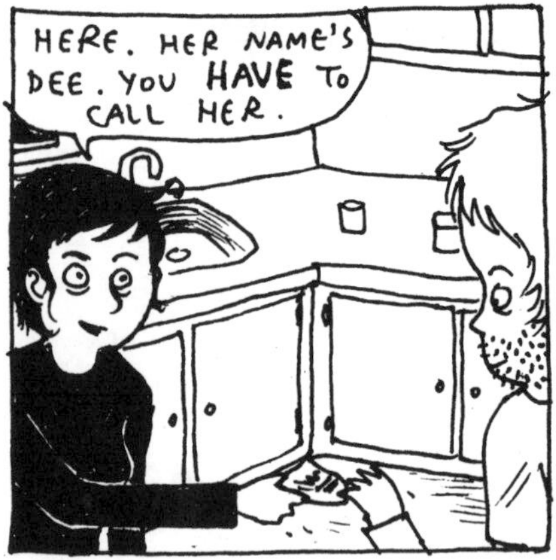
HERE. HER NAME'S DEE. YOU HAVE TO CALL HER.

SATURDAY

JANUARY 3

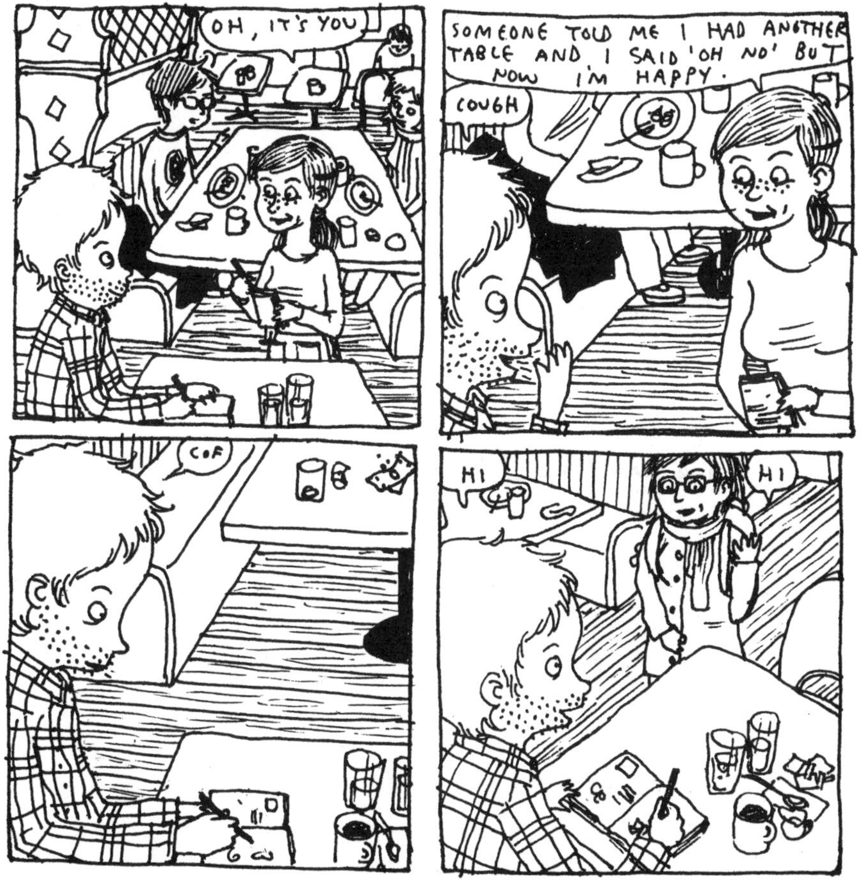
OH, IT'S YOU
SOMEONE TOLD ME I HAD ANOTHER TABLE AND I SAID 'OH NO' BUT NOW I'M HAPPY.
COUGH
COF
HI
HI

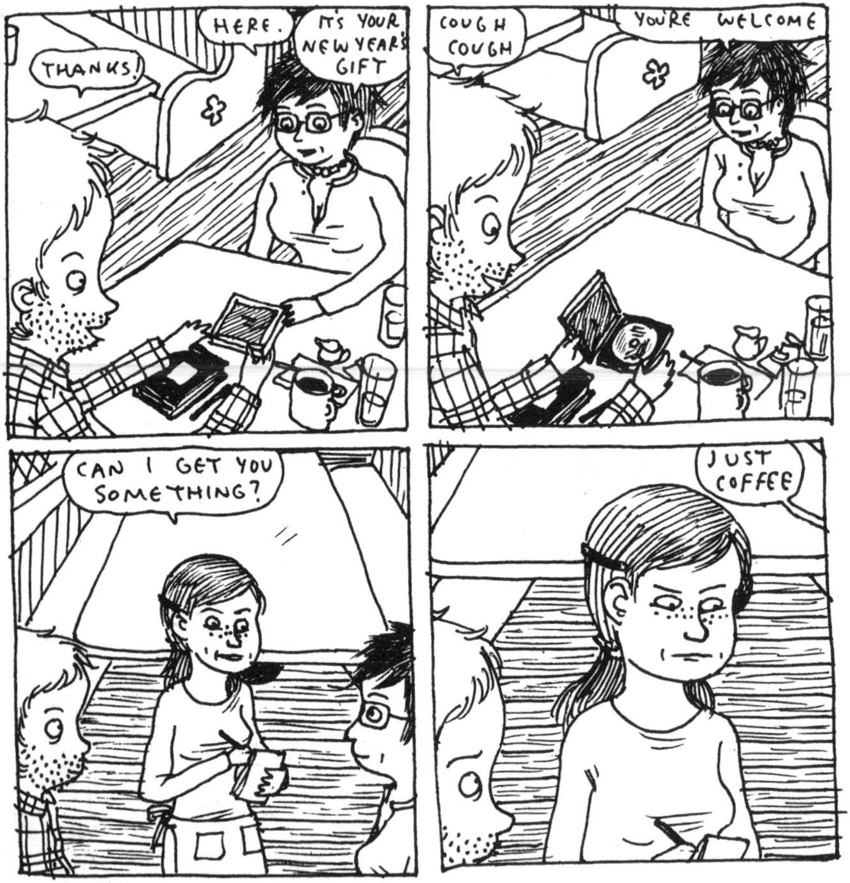
THANKS!
HERE.
IT'S YOUR NEW YEAR'S GIFT
COUGH COUGH
YOU'RE WELCOME
CAN I GET YOU SOMETHING?
JUST COFFEE

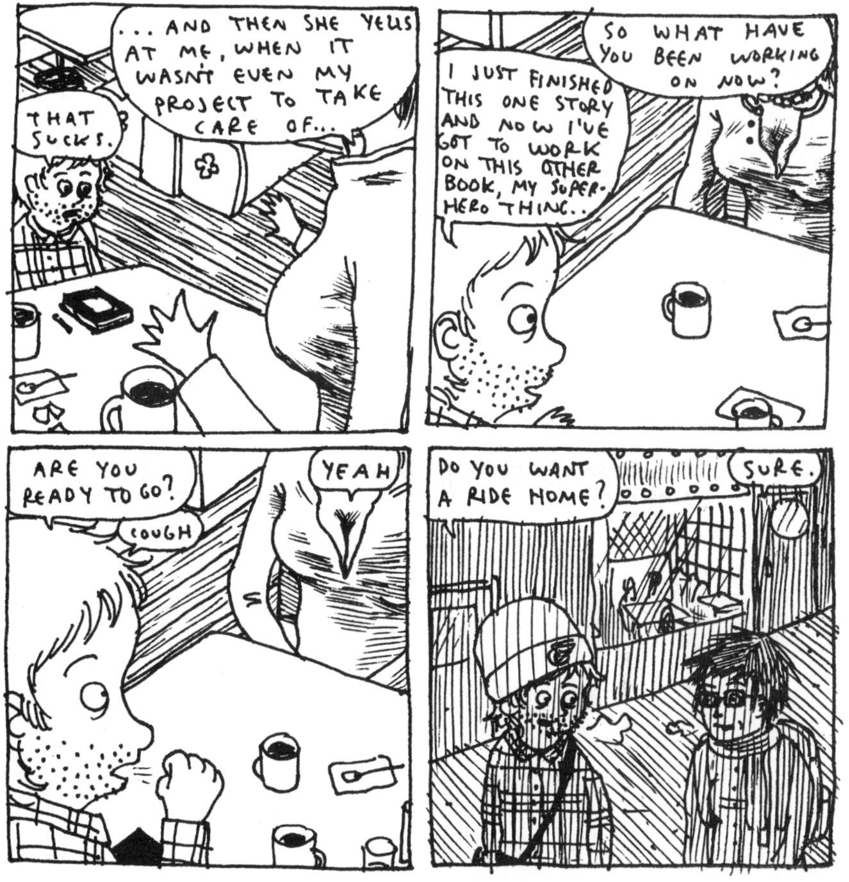
... AND THEN SHE YELLS AT ME, WHEN IT WASN'T EVEN MY PROJECT TO TAKE CARE OF...
THAT SUCKS.
SO WHAT HAVE YOU BEEN WORKING ON NOW?
I JUST FINISHED THIS ONE STORY AND NOW I'VE GOT TO WORK ON THIS OTHER BOOK, MY SUPER-HERO THING..
ARE YOU READY TO GO?
YEAH
COUGH
DO YOU WANT A RIDE HOME?
SURE.

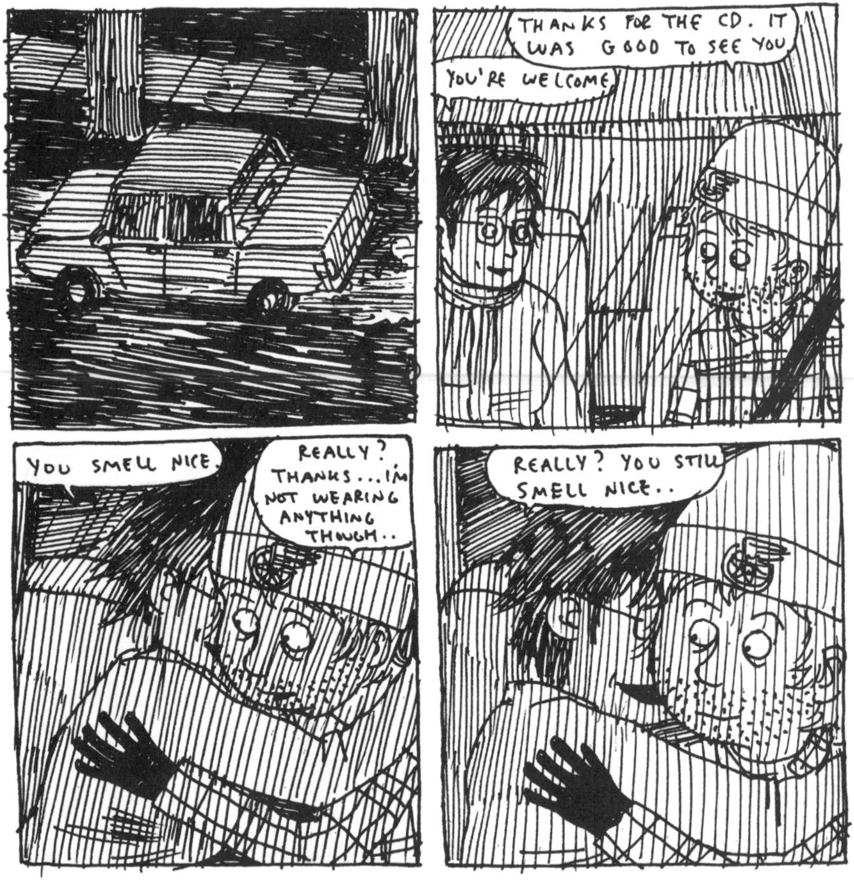
THANKS FOR THE CD. IT WAS GOOD TO SEE YOU
YOU'RE WELCOME
YOU SMELL NICE.
REALLY? THANKS...I'M NOT WEARING ANYTHING THOUGH..
REALLY? YOU STILL SMELL NICE..

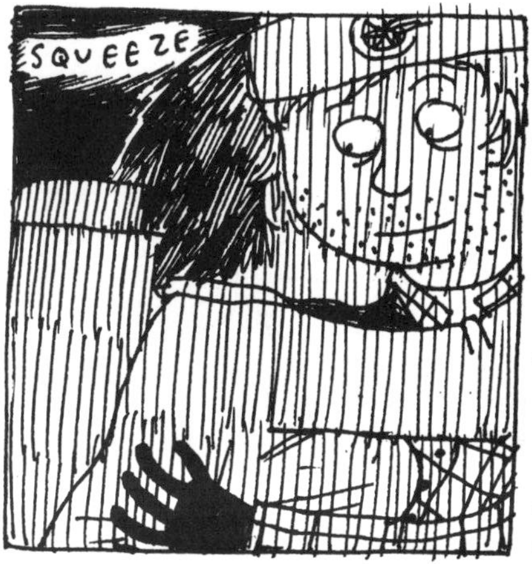
SQUEEZE

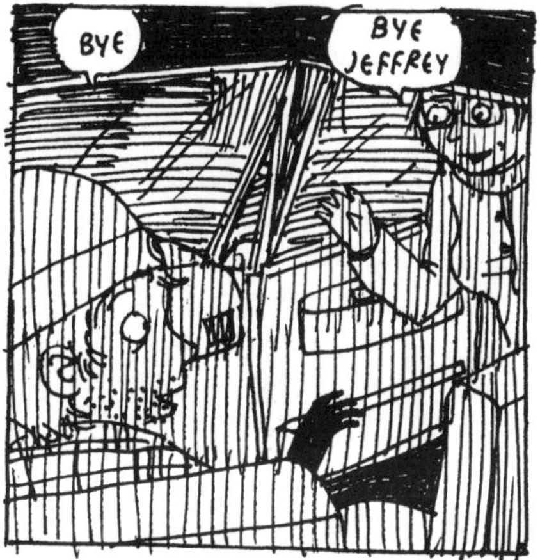
BYE
BYE JEFFREY

SUNDAY

JANUARY 4

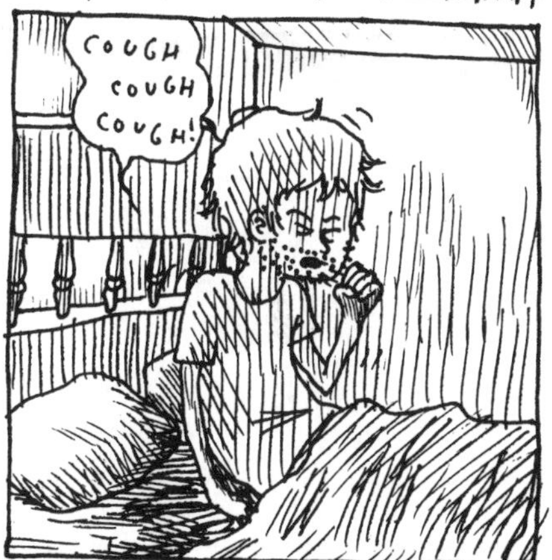
COUGH COUGH COUGH!

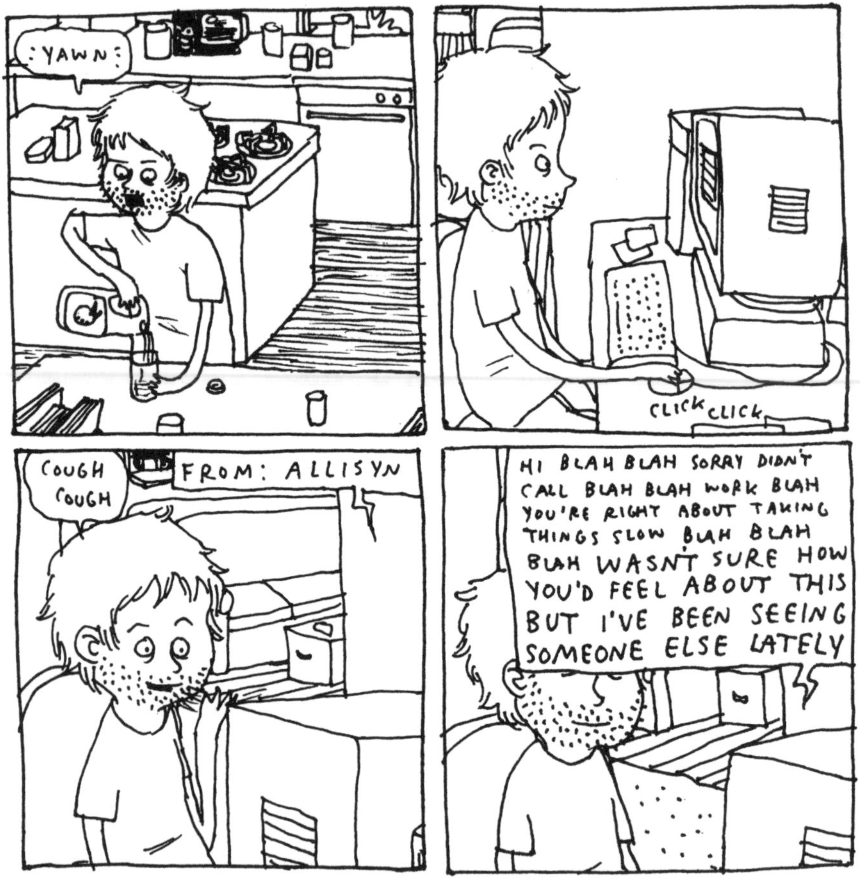
YAWN
CLICK CLICK
COUGH COUGH
FROM: ALLISYN
HI BLAH BLAH SORRY DIDN'T CALL BLAH BLAH WORK BLAH YOU'RE RIGHT ABOUT TAKING THINGS SLOW BLAH BLAH BLAH WASN'T SURE HOW YOU'D FEEL ABOUT THIS BUT I'VE BEEN SEEING SOMEONE ELSE LATELY

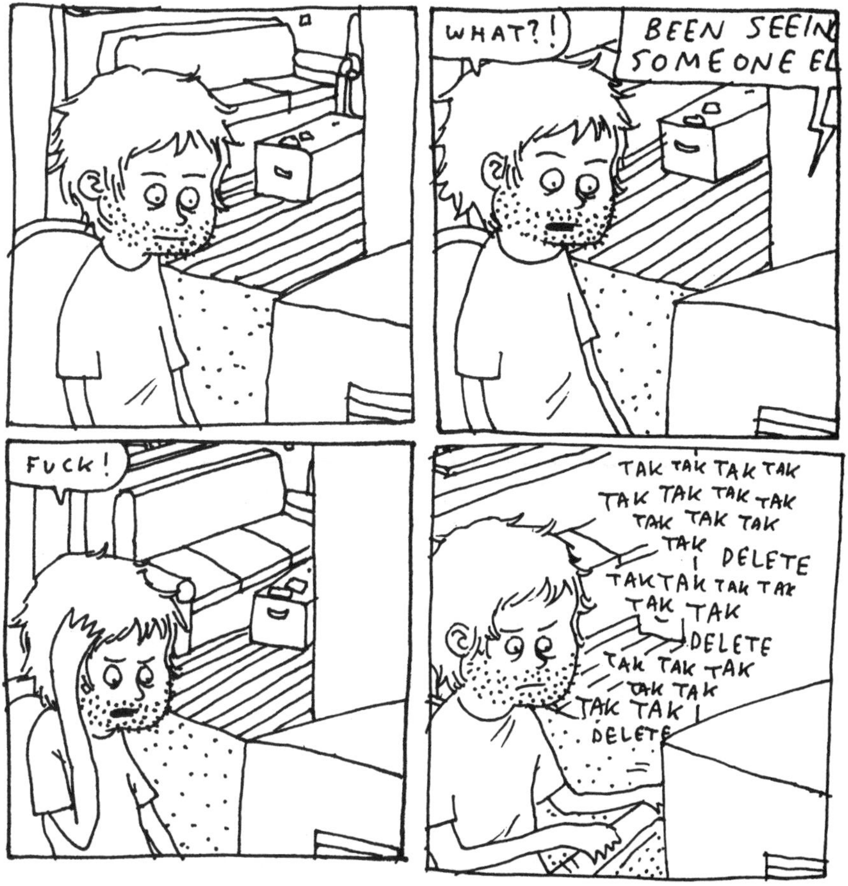
WHAT?!
BEEN SEEIN
SOMEONE EL
FUCK!
TAK TAK TAK TAK
TAK TAK TAK TAK
TAK TAK TAK
TAK DELETE
TAK TAK TAK TAK
TAK TAK
DELETE
TAK TAK TAK
TAK TAK
TAK TAK
DELETE

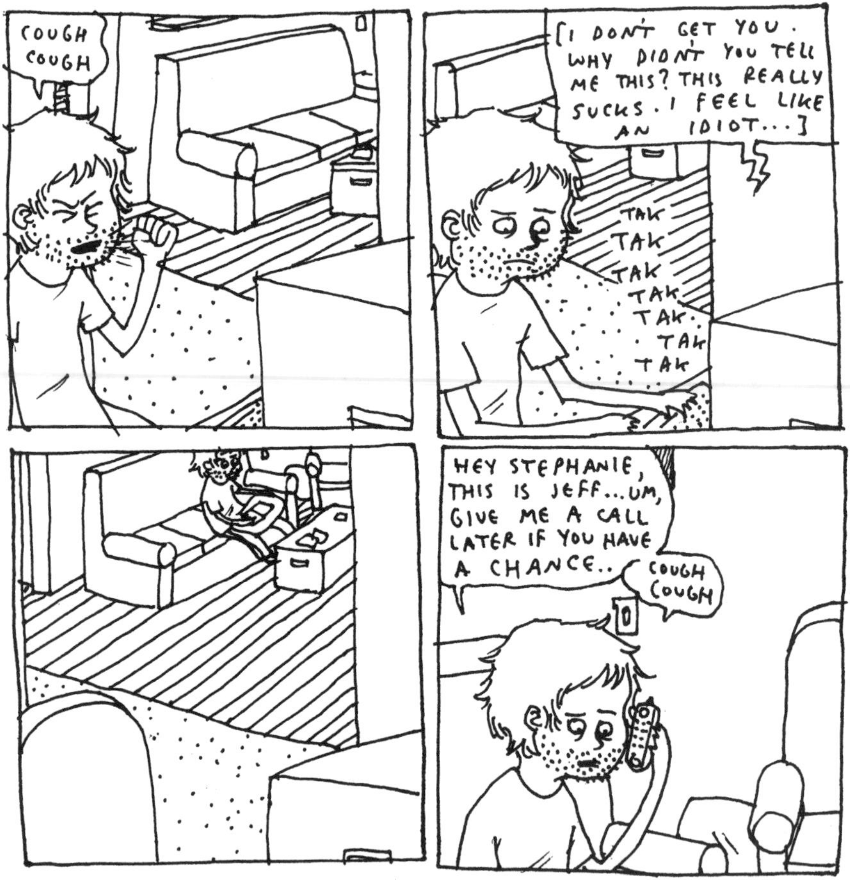
COUGH COUGH
[I DON'T GET YOU. WHY DIDN'T YOU TELL ME THIS? THIS REALLY SUCKS. I FEEL LIKE AN IDIOT...]
TAK TAK TAK TAK TAK TAK TAK
HEY STEPHANIE, THIS IS JEFF...UM, GIVE ME A CALL LATER IF YOU HAVE A CHANCE..
COUGH COUGH

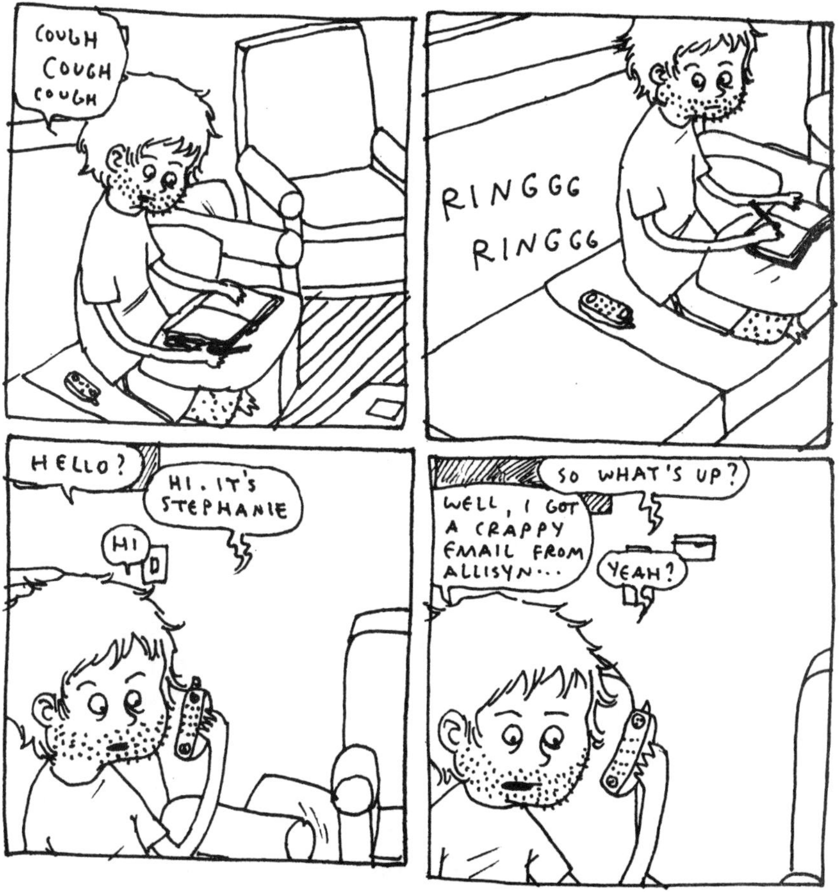
COUGH
COUGH
COUGH
RINGGG
RINGGG
HELLO?
HI. IT'S STEPHANIE
HI
SO WHAT'S UP?
WELL, I GOT A CRAPPY EMAIL FROM ALLISYN...
YEAH?

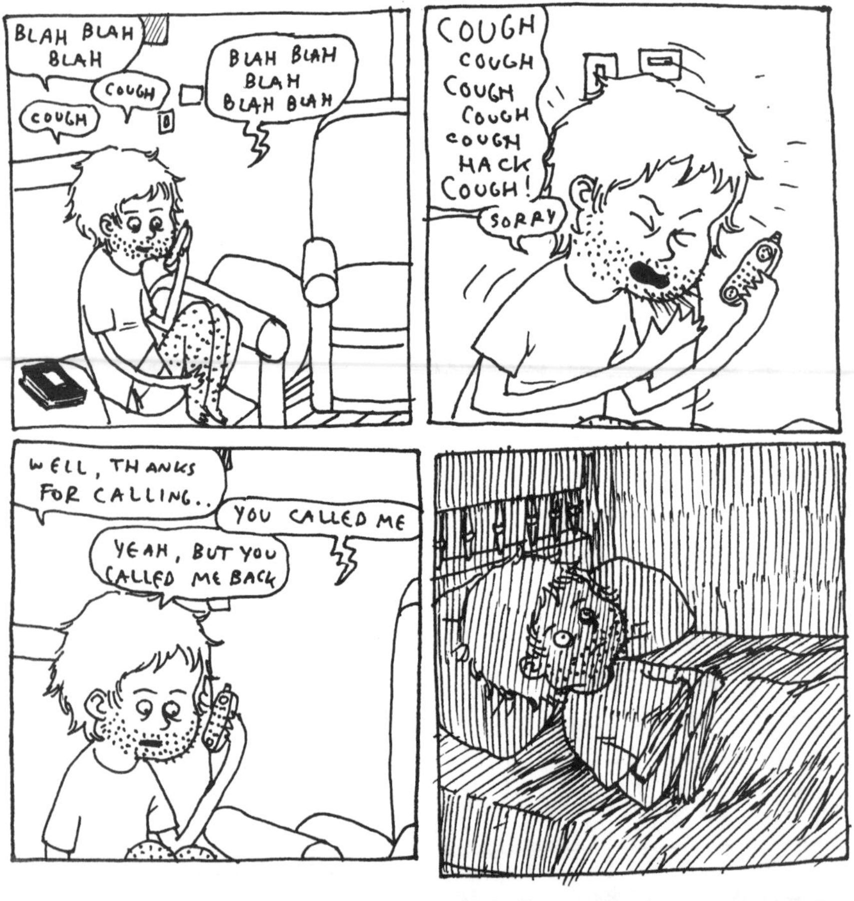
BLAH BLAH BLAH
COUGH
COUGH
BLAH BLAH BLAH BLAH BLAH
COUGH COUGH COUGH COUGH COUGH HACK COUGH!
SORRY
WELL, THANKS FOR CALLING..
YOU CALLED ME
YEAH, BUT YOU CALLED ME BACK

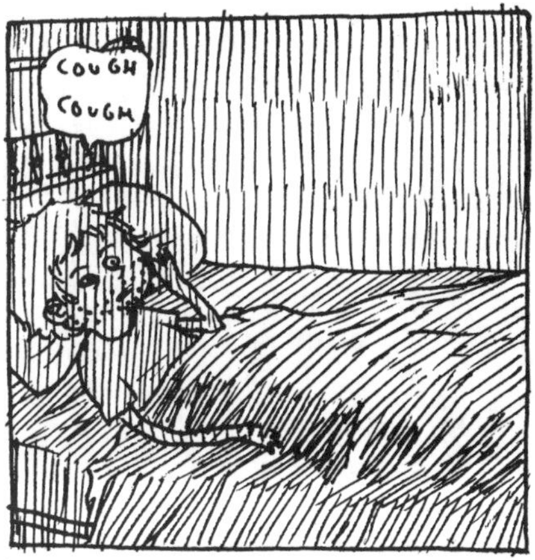
COUGH
COUGH

MONDAY

JANUARY 5

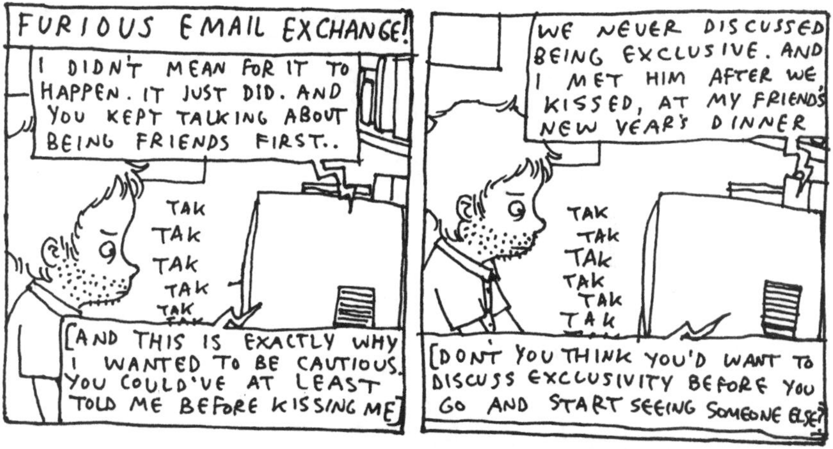
FURIOUS EMAIL EXCHANGE!
I DIDN'T MEAN FOR IT TO HAPPEN. IT JUST DID. AND YOU KEPT TALKING ABOUT BEING FRIENDS FIRST..
TAK
TAK
TAK
TAK
TAK
[AND THIS IS EXACTLY WHY I WANTED TO BE CAUTIOUS. YOU COULD'VE AT LEAST TOLD ME BEFORE KISSING ME]
WE NEVER DISCUSSED BEING EXCLUSIVE. AND I MET HIM AFTER WE KISSED, AT MY FRIEND'S NEW YEAR'S DINNER
TAK
TAK
TAK
TAK
TAK
TAK
[DON'T YOU THINK YOU'D WANT TO DISCUSS EXCLUSIVITY BEFORE YOU GO AND START SEEING SOMEONE ELSE?]

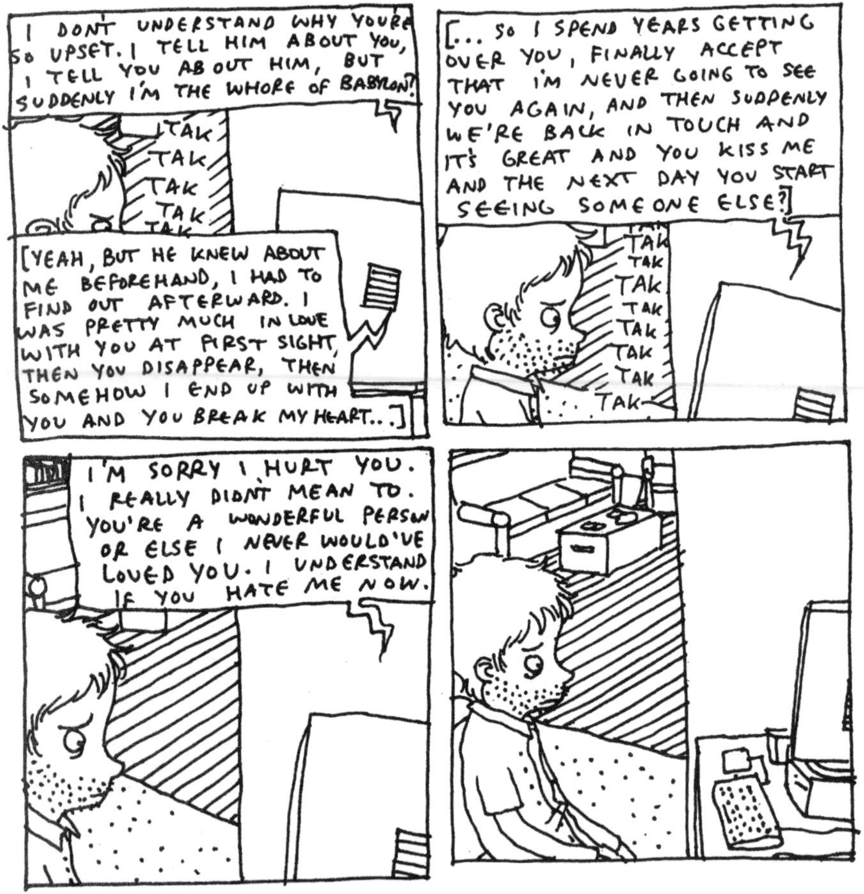
I DONT UNDERSTAND WHY YOU'RE SO UPSET. I TELL HIM ABOUT YOU, I TELL YOU ABOUT HIM, BUT SUDDENLY I'M THE WHORE OF BABYLON?
TAK TAK TAK TAK TAK
[YEAH, BUT HE KNEW ABOUT ME BEFOREHAND, I HAD TO FIND OUT AFTERWARD. I WAS PRETTY MUCH IN LOVE WITH YOU AT FIRST SIGHT, THEN YOU DISAPPEAR, THEN SOMEHOW I END UP WITH YOU AND YOU BREAK MY HEART...]
[... SO I SPEND YEARS GETTING OVER YOU, FINALLY ACCEPT THAT I'M NEVER GOING TO SEE YOU AGAIN, AND THEN SUDDENLY WE'RE BACK IN TOUCH AND IT'S GREAT AND YOU KISS ME AND THE NEXT DAY YOU START SEEING SOMEONE ELSE?]
TAK TAK TAK TAK TAK TAK TAK TAK
I'M SORRY I HURT YOU. I REALLY DIDNT MEAN TO. YOU'RE A WONDERFUL PERSON OR ELSE I NEVER WOULD'VE LOVED YOU. I UNDERSTAND IF YOU HATE ME NOW.

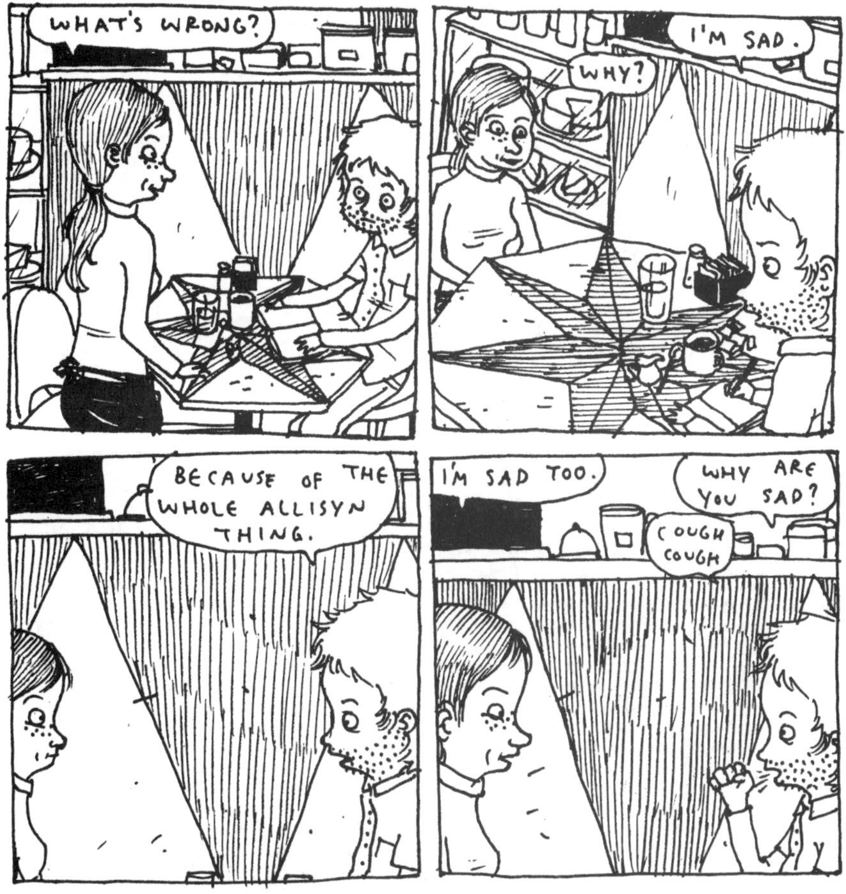
WHAT'S WRONG?
I'M SAD.
WHY?
BECAUSE OF THE WHOLE ALLISYN THING.
I'M SAD TOO.
WHY ARE YOU SAD?
COUGH COUGH

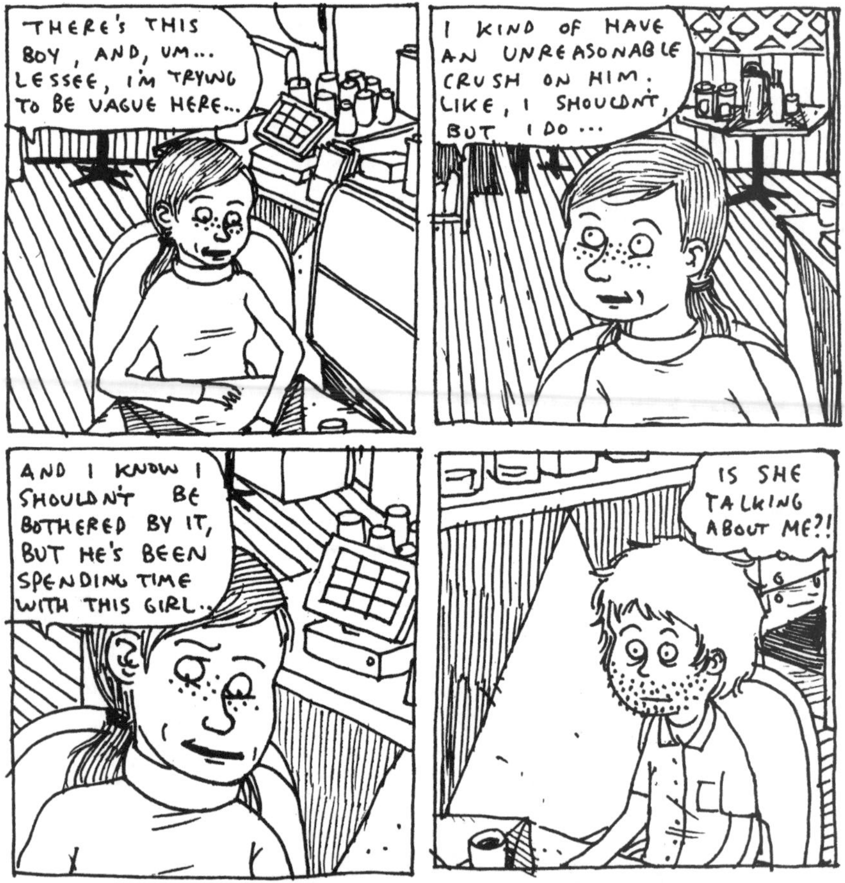
THERE'S THIS BOY, AND, UM... LESSEE, I'M TRYING TO BE VAGUE HERE...
I KIND OF HAVE AN UNREASONABLE CRUSH ON HIM. LIKE, I SHOULDN'T, BUT I DO...
AND I KNOW I SHOULDN'T BE BOTHERED BY IT, BUT HE'S BEEN SPENDING TIME WITH THIS GIRL..
IS SHE TALKING ABOUT ME?!

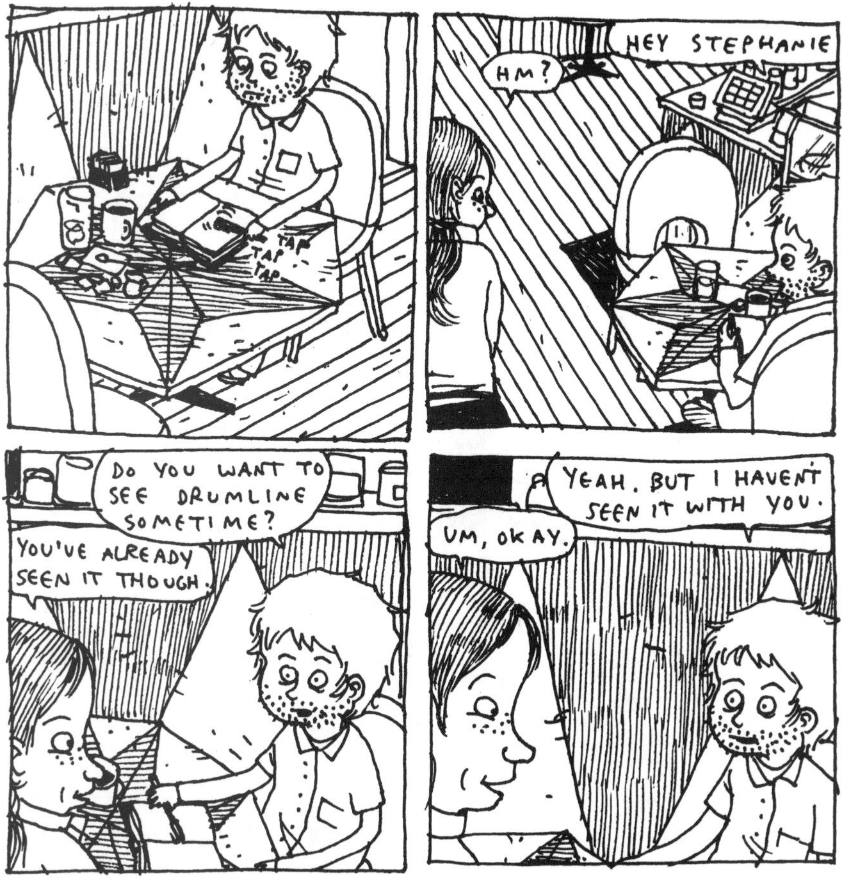
TAP
TAP
TAP
HEY STEPHANIE
HM?
DO YOU WANT TO SEE DRUMLINE SOMETIME?
YOU'VE ALREADY SEEN IT THOUGH.
YEAH. BUT I HAVENT SEEN IT WITH YOU.
UM, OKAY.

TUESDAY

JANUARY 6

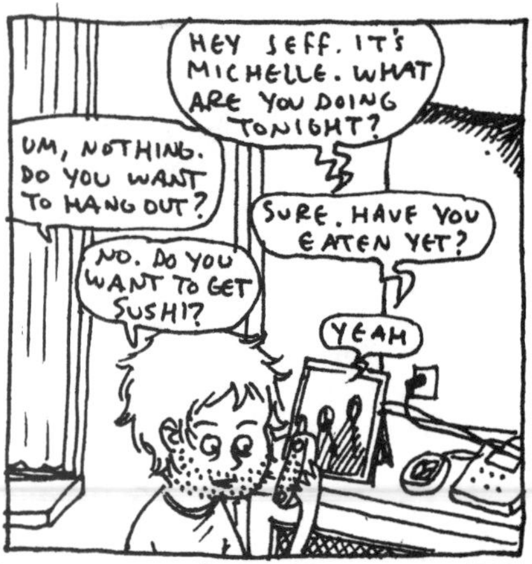
HEY JEFF. IT'S MICHELLE. WHAT ARE YOU DOING TONIGHT?
UM, NOTHING. DO YOU WANT TO HANG OUT?
SURE. HAVE YOU EATEN YET?
NO. DO YOU WANT TO GET SUSHI?
YEAH

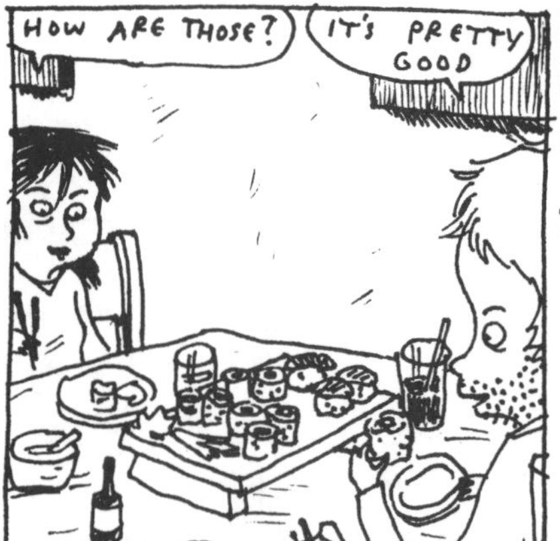
HOW ARE THOSE?
IT'S PRETTY GOOD

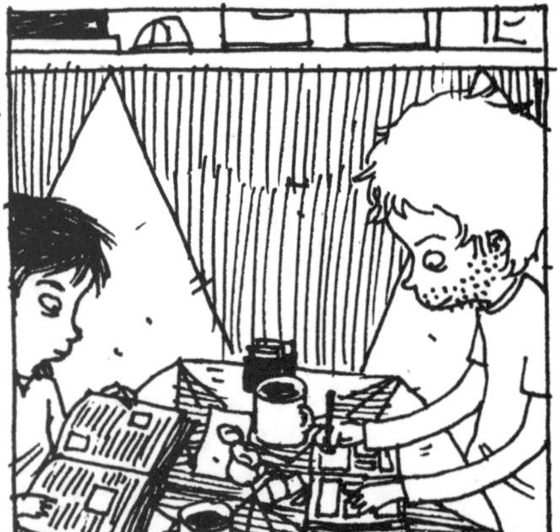

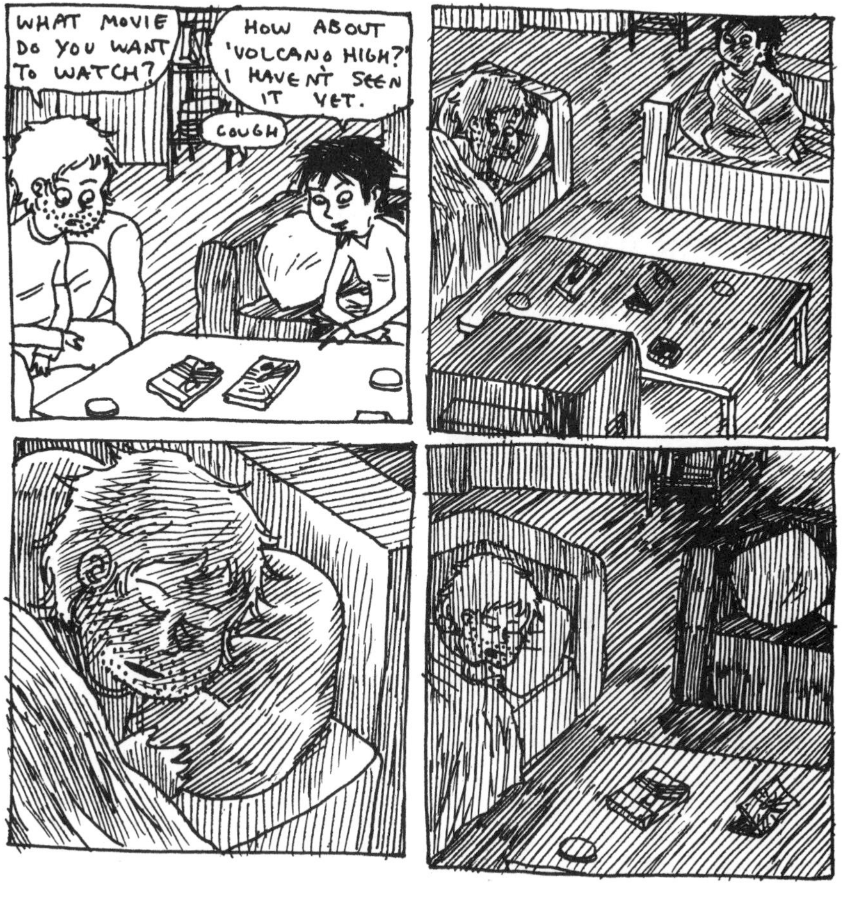
WHAT MOVIE DO YOU WANT TO WATCH?
HOW ABOUT 'VOLCANO HIGH?' I HAVEN'T SEEN IT YET.
COUGH

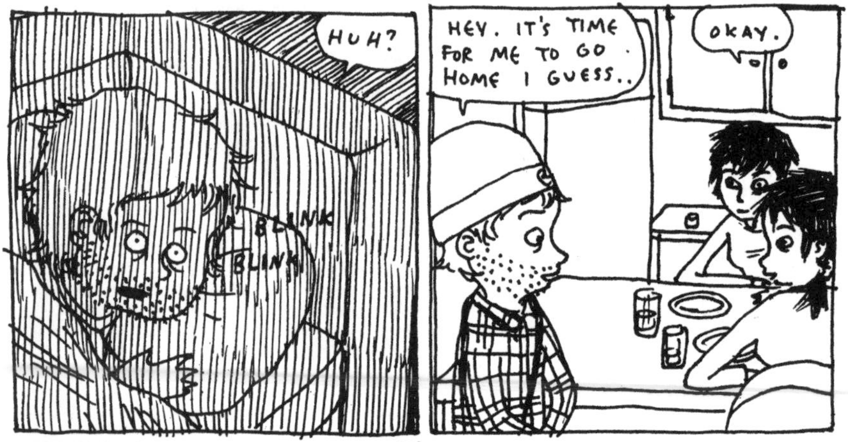
HUH?
BLINK
BLINK
HEY. IT'S TIME FOR ME TO GO HOME I GUESS..
OKAY.

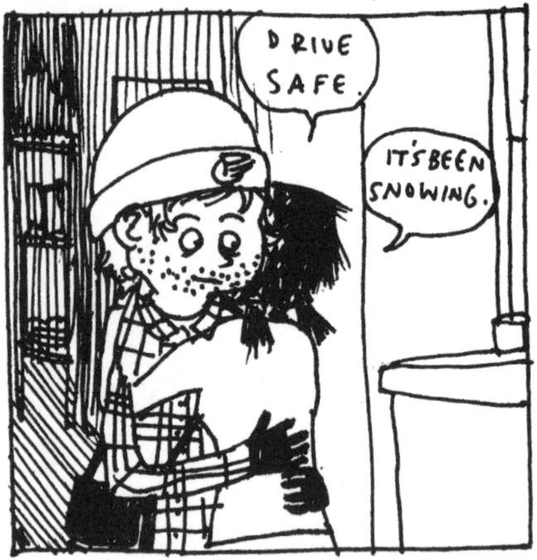
DRIVE SAFE.
IT'S BEEN SNOWING.

WEDNESDAY

JANUARY 7

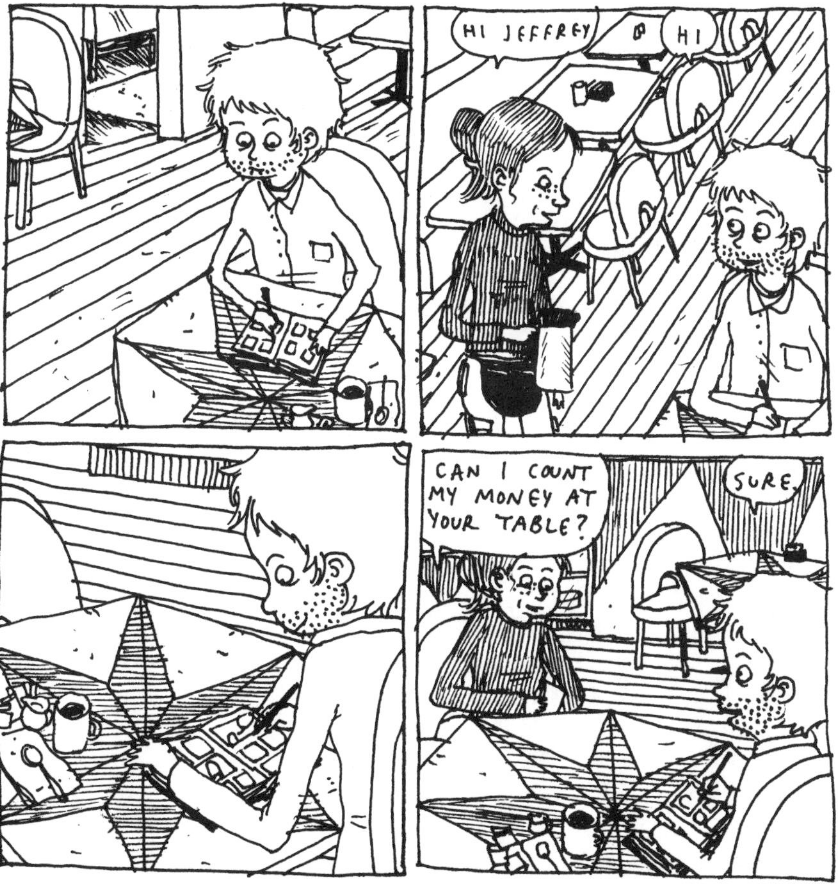
HI JEFFREY
HI
CAN I COUNT MY MONEY AT YOUR TABLE?
SURE.

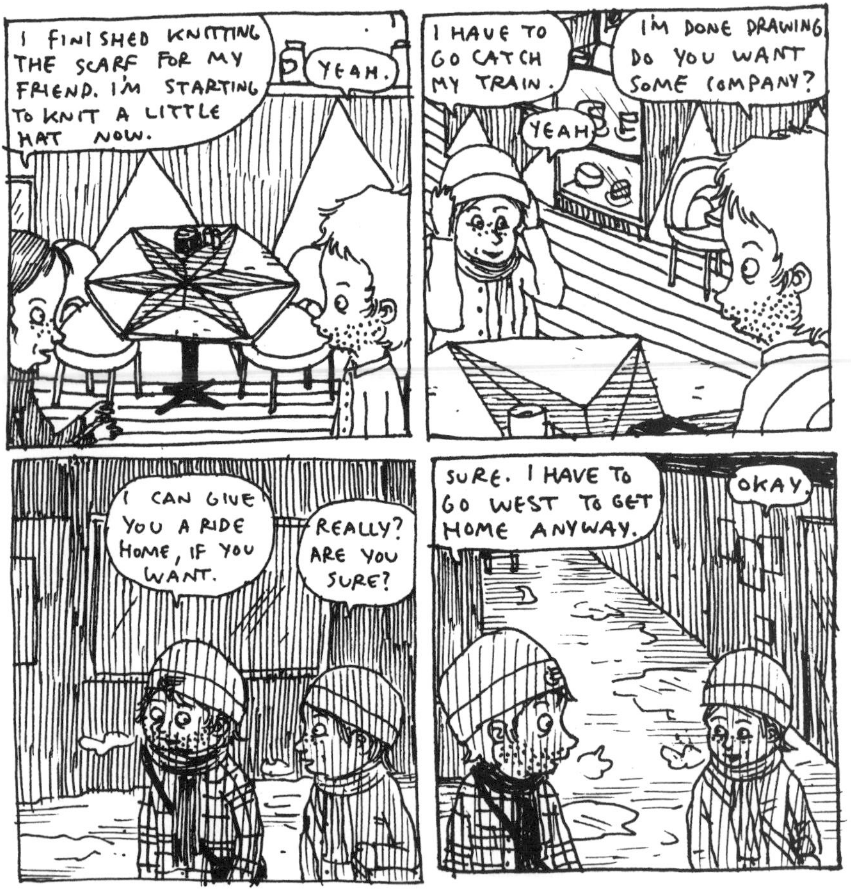
I FINISHED KNITTING THE SCARF FOR MY FRIEND. I'M STARTING TO KNIT A LITTLE HAT NOW.
YEAH.
I HAVE TO GO CATCH MY TRAIN.
YEAH
I'M DONE DRAWING DO YOU WANT SOME COMPANY?
I CAN GIVE YOU A RIDE HOME, IF YOU WANT.
REALLY? ARE YOU SURE?
SURE. I HAVE TO GO WEST TO GET HOME ANYWAY.
OKAY.

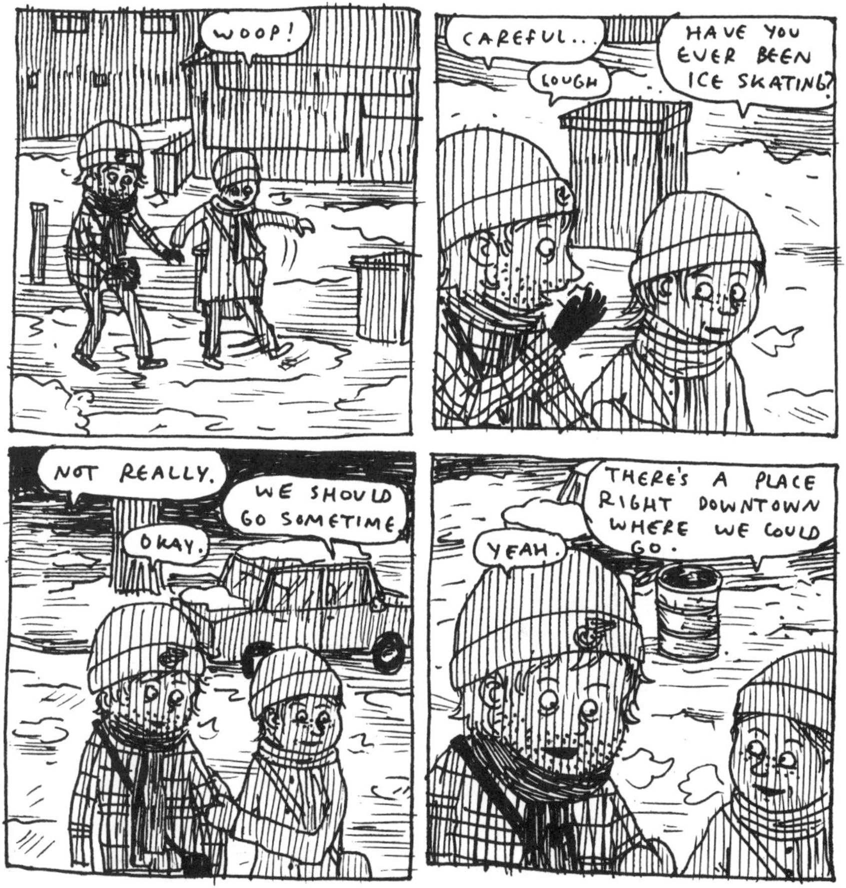
WOOP!
CAREFUL..
COUGH
HAVE YOU EVER BEEN ICE SKATING?
NOT REALLY.
WE SHOULD GO SOMETIME.
OKAY.
THERE'S A PLACE RIGHT DOWNTOWN WHERE WE COULD GO.
YEAH.

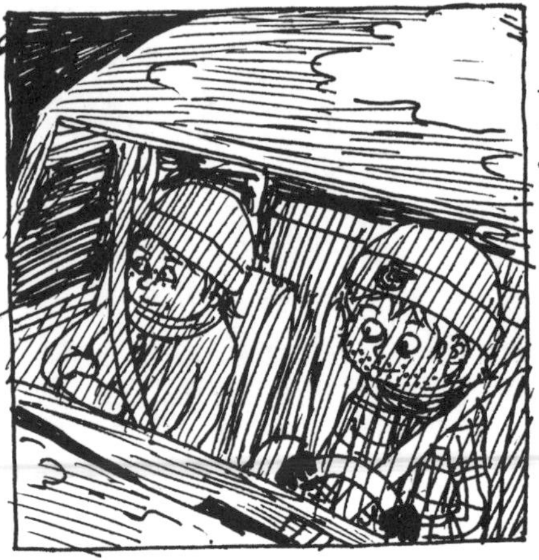

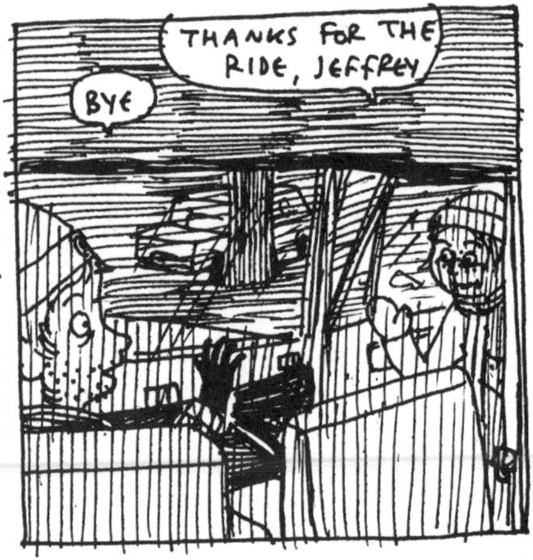
THANKS FOR THE RIDE, JEFFREY
BYE

THURSDAY

JANUARY 8

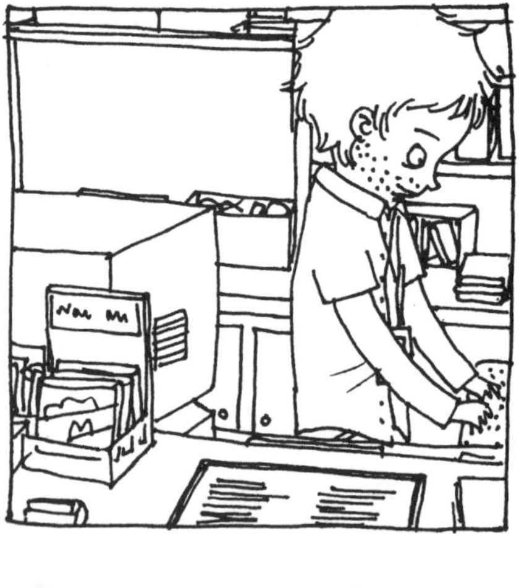

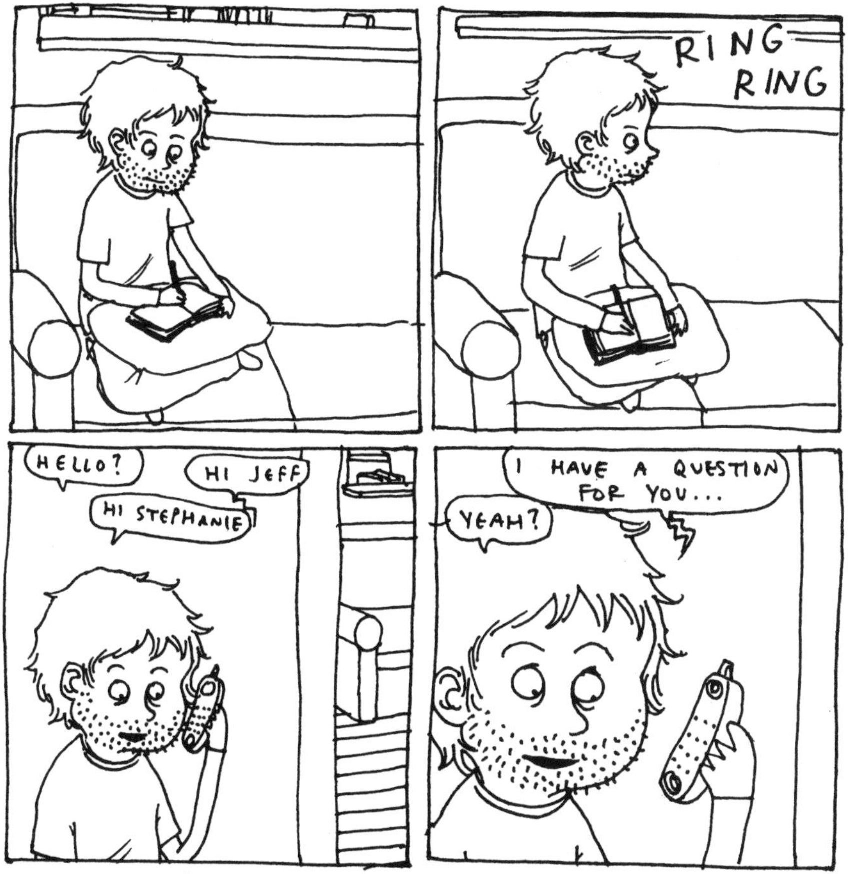
RING
RING
HELLO?
HI JEFF
HI STEPHANIE!
I HAVE A QUESTION FOR YOU...
YEAH?

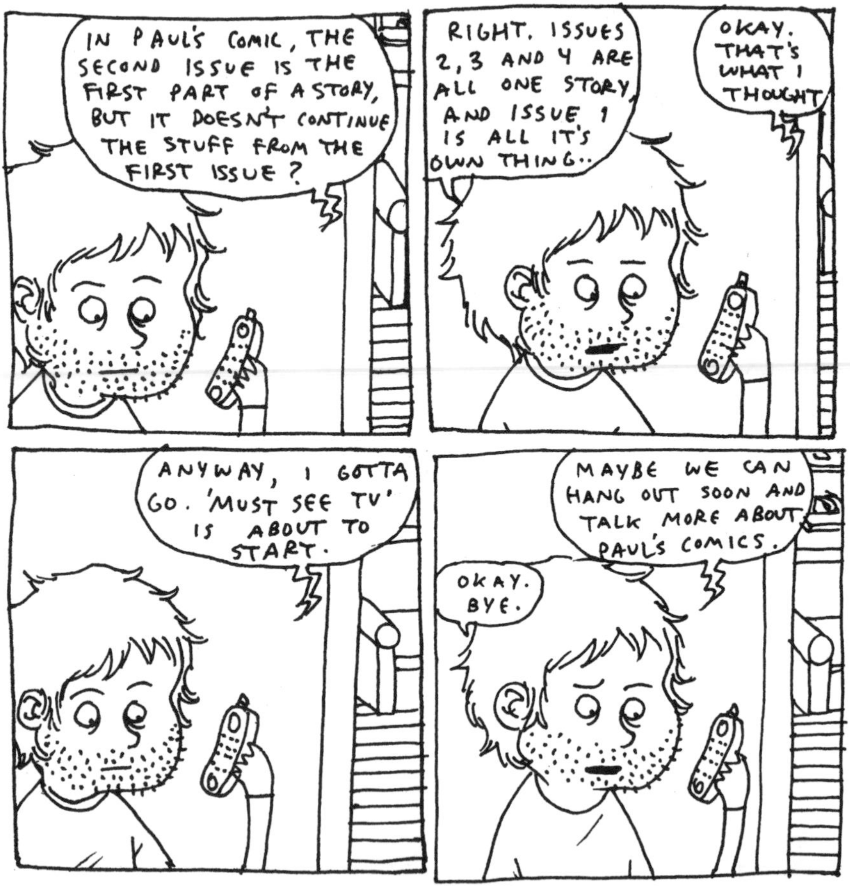
IN PAUL'S COMIC, THE SECOND ISSUE IS THE FIRST PART OF A STORY, BUT IT DOESN'T CONTINUE THE STUFF FROM THE FIRST ISSUE?
RIGHT. ISSUES 2, 3 AND 4 ARE ALL ONE STORY, AND ISSUE 1 IS ALL IT'S OWN THING..
OKAY. THAT'S WHAT I THOUGHT
ANYWAY, I GOTTA GO. 'MUST SEE TV' IS ABOUT TO START.
MAYBE WE CAN HANG OUT SOON AND TALK MORE ABOUT PAUL'S COMICS.
OKAY. BYE.

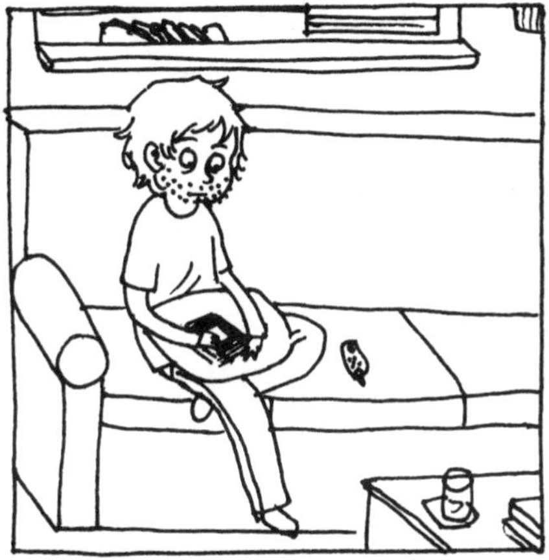

FRIDAY

JANUARY 9

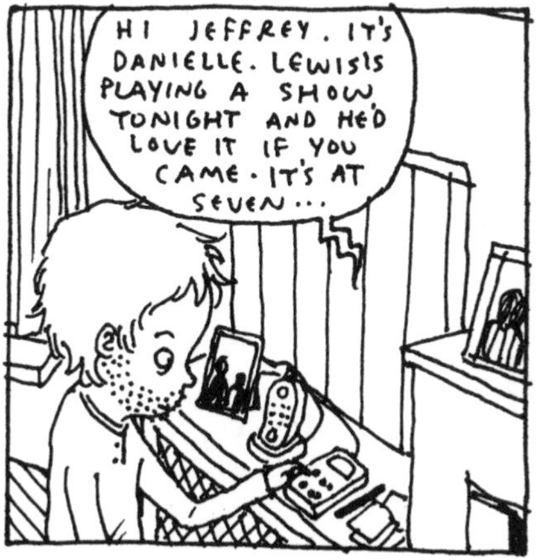
HI JEFFREY. IT'S DANIELLE. LEWIS'S PLAYING A SHOW TONIGHT AND HE'D LOVE IT IF YOU CAME. IT'S AT SEVEN...

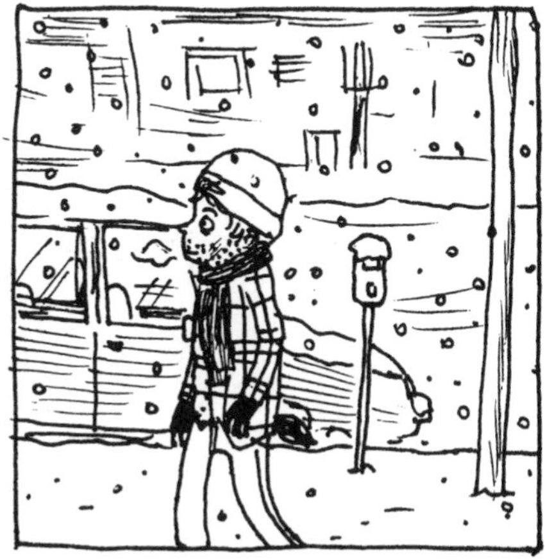

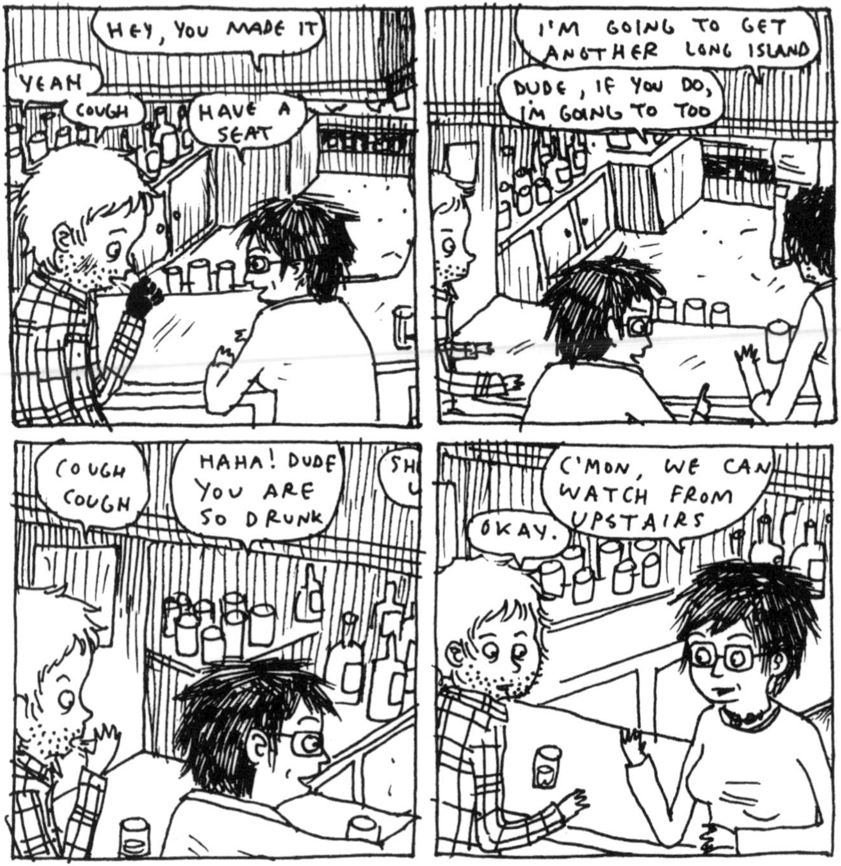
HEY, YOU MADE IT
YEAH
COUGH
HAVE A SEAT
I'M GOING TO GET ANOTHER LONG ISLAND
DUDE, IF YOU DO, I'M GOING TO TOO
COUGH COUGH
HAHA! DUDE YOU ARE SO DRUNK
C'MON, WE CAN WATCH FROM UPSTAIRS
OKAY.

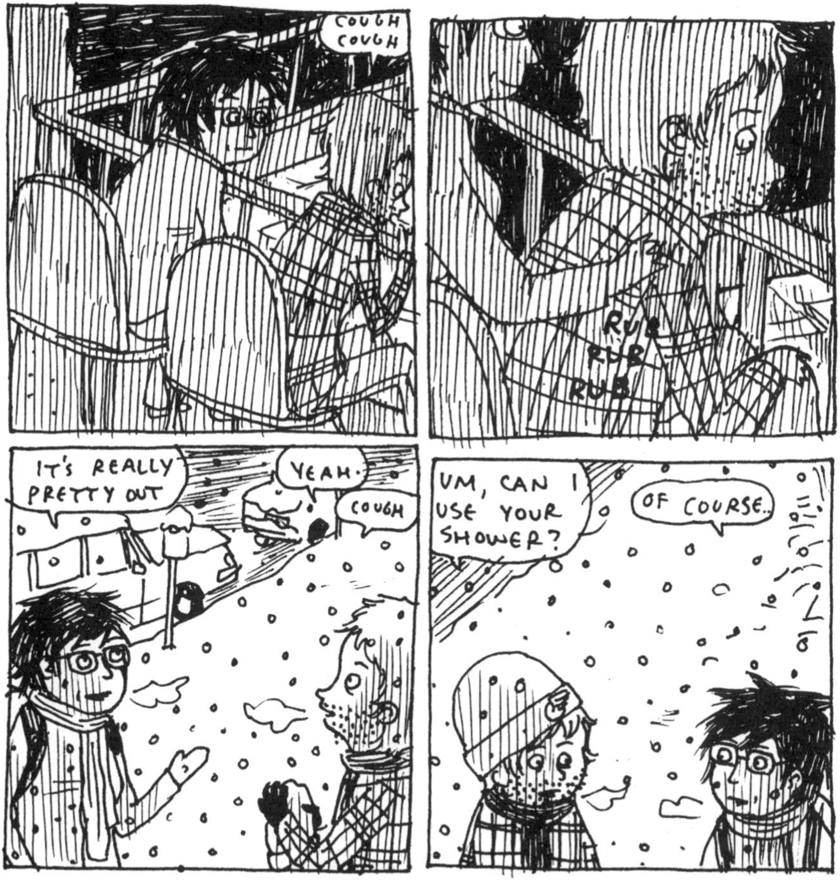
COUGH
COUGH
RUB
RUB
RUB
IT'S REALLY PRETTY OUT
YEAH.
COUGH
UM, CAN I USE YOUR SHOWER?
OF COURSE.

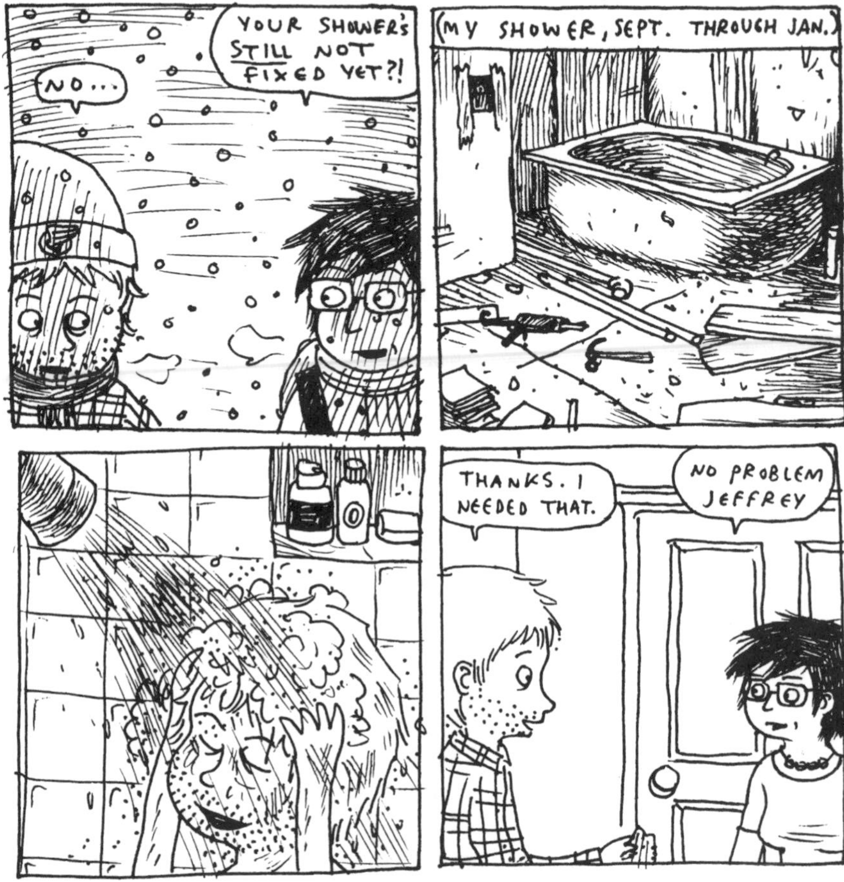
YOUR SHOWER'S STILL NOT FIXED YET?!
NO...
(MY SHOWER, SEPT. THROUGH JAN.)
THANKS. I NEEDED THAT.
NO PROBLEM JEFFREY

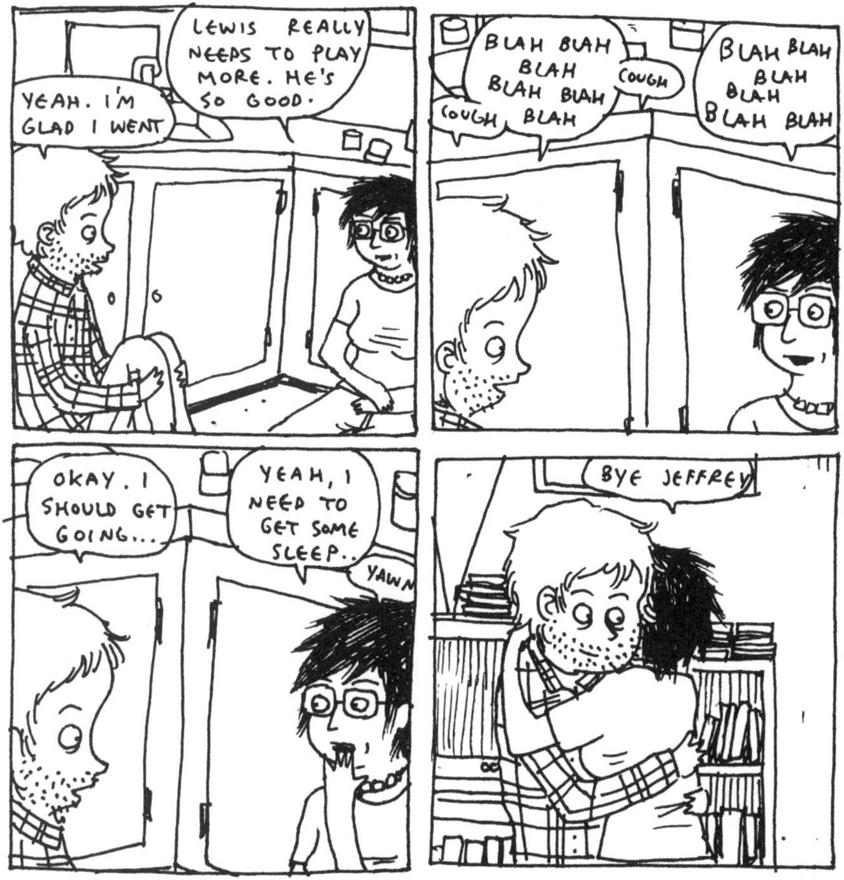
YEAH. I'M GLAD I WENT
LEWIS REALLY NEEDS TO PLAY MORE. HE'S SO GOOD.
COUGH
BLAH BLAH BLAH BLAH BLAH BLAH
COUGH
BLAH BLAH BLAH BLAH BLAH BLAH
OKAY. I SHOULD GET GOING...
YEAH, I NEED TO GET SOME SLEEP..
YAWN
BYE JEFFREY

SATURDAY

JANUARY 10

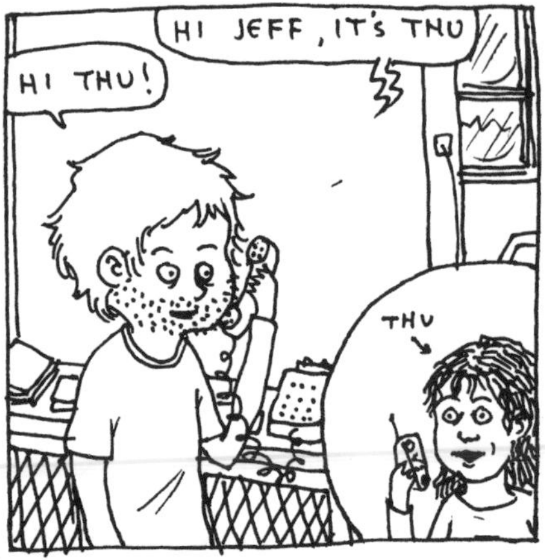
HI JEFF, IT'S THU
HI THU!
THU

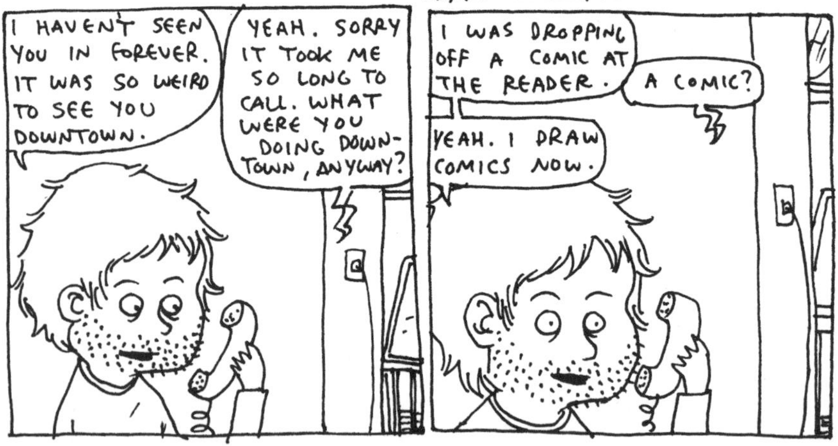
I HAVEN'T SEEN YOU IN FOREVER. IT WAS SO WEIRD TO SEE YOU DOWNTOWN.
YEAH. SORRY IT TOOK ME SO LONG TO CALL. WHAT WERE YOU DOING DOWNTOWN, ANYWAY?
I WAS DROPPING OFF A COMIC AT THE READER.
A COMIC?
YEAH. I DRAW COMICS NOW.

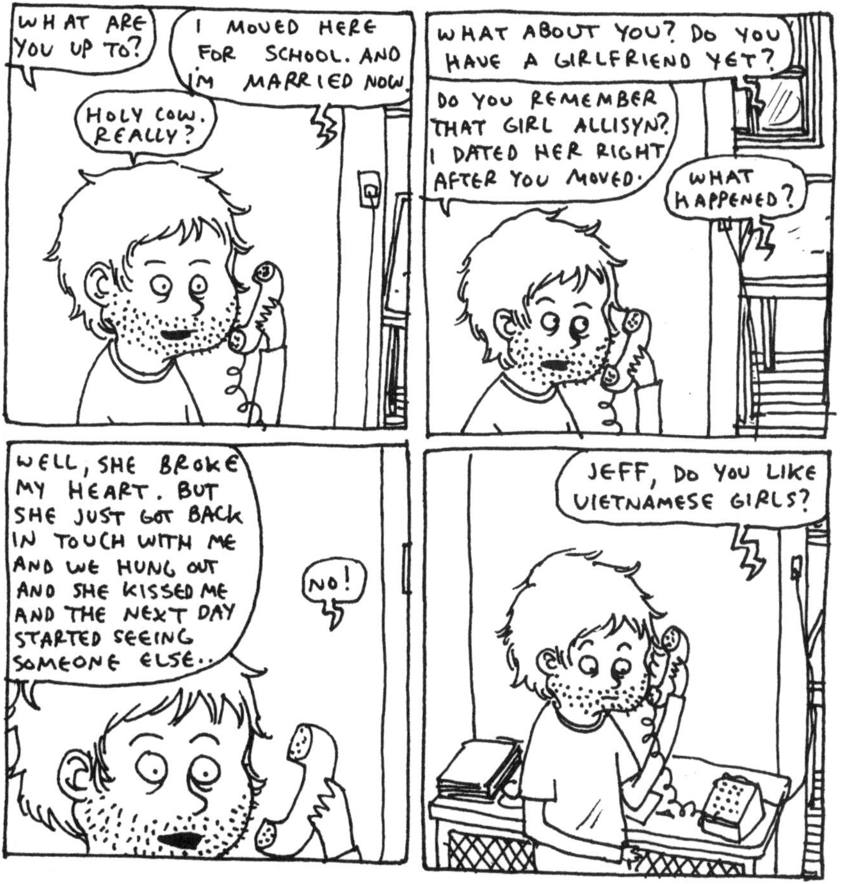
WHAT ARE YOU UP TO?
I MOVED HERE FOR SCHOOL. AND I'M MARRIED NOW.
HOLY COW. REALLY?
WHAT ABOUT YOU? DO YOU HAVE A GIRLFRIEND YET?
DO YOU REMEMBER THAT GIRL ALLISYN? I DATED HER RIGHT AFTER YOU MOVED.
WHAT HAPPENED?
WELL, SHE BROKE MY HEART. BUT SHE JUST GOT BACK IN TOUCH WITH ME AND WE HUNG OUT AND SHE KISSED ME AND THE NEXT DAY STARTED SEEING SOMEONE ELSE...
NO!
JEFF, DO YOU LIKE VIETNAMESE GIRLS?

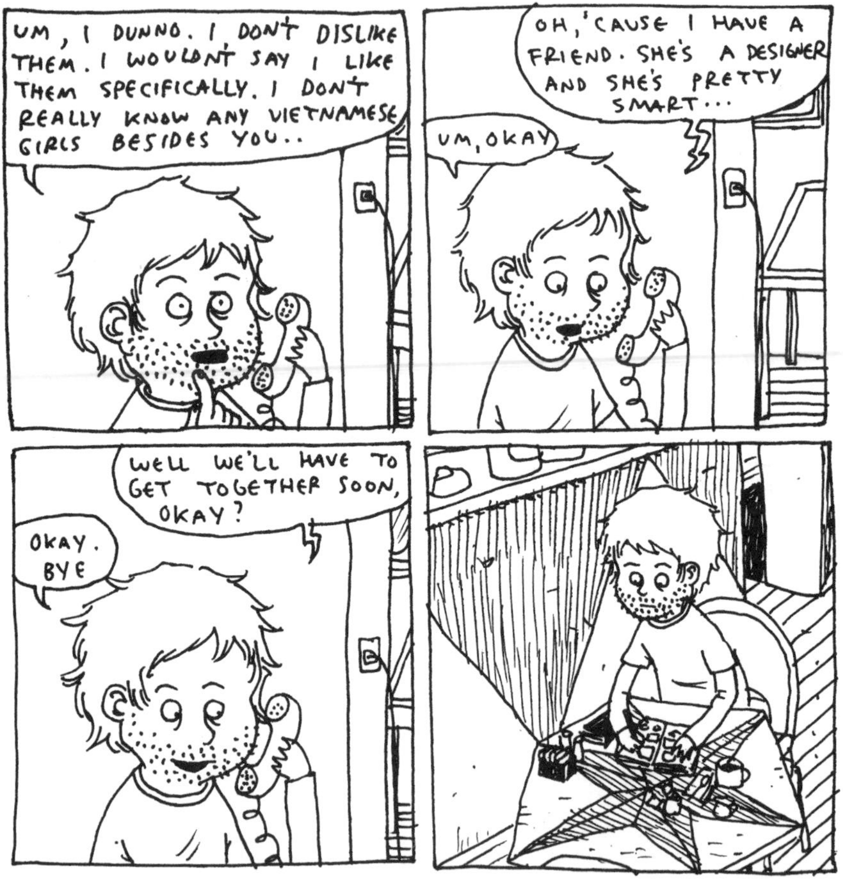
UM, I DUNNO. I DON'T DISLIKE THEM. I WOULDN'T SAY I LIKE THEM SPECIFICALLY. I DON'T REALLY KNOW ANY VIETNAMESE GIRLS BESIDES YOU..
OH, 'CAUSE I HAVE A FRIEND. SHE'S A DESIGNER AND SHE'S PRETTY SMART...
UM, OKAY
WELL WE'LL HAVE TO GET TOGETHER SOON, OKAY?
OKAY. BYE

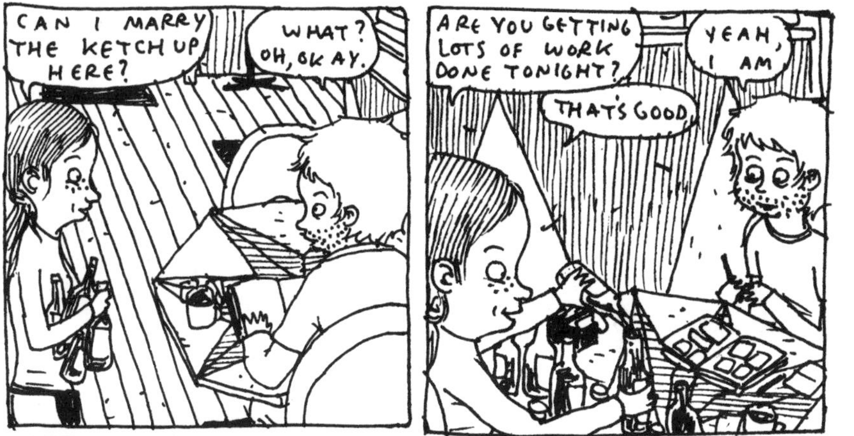
CAN I MARRY THE KETCHUP HERE?
WHAT? OH, OKAY.
ARE YOU GETTING LOTS OF WORK DONE TONIGHT?
YEAH, I AM
THAT'S GOOD

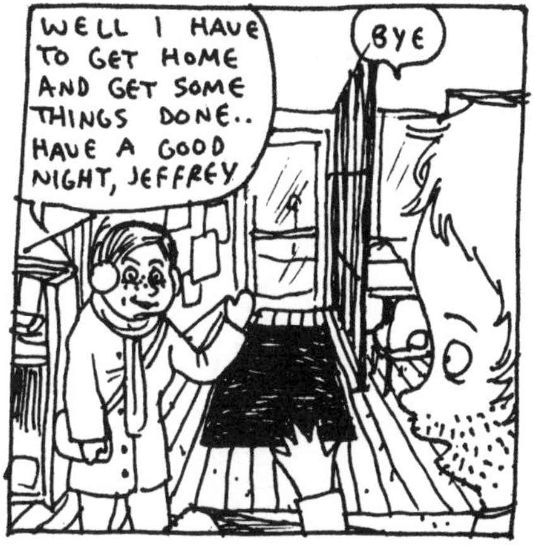
WELL I HAVE TO GET HOME AND GET SOME THINGS DONE.. HAVE A GOOD NIGHT, JEFFREY
BYE

SUNDAY

JANUARY 11

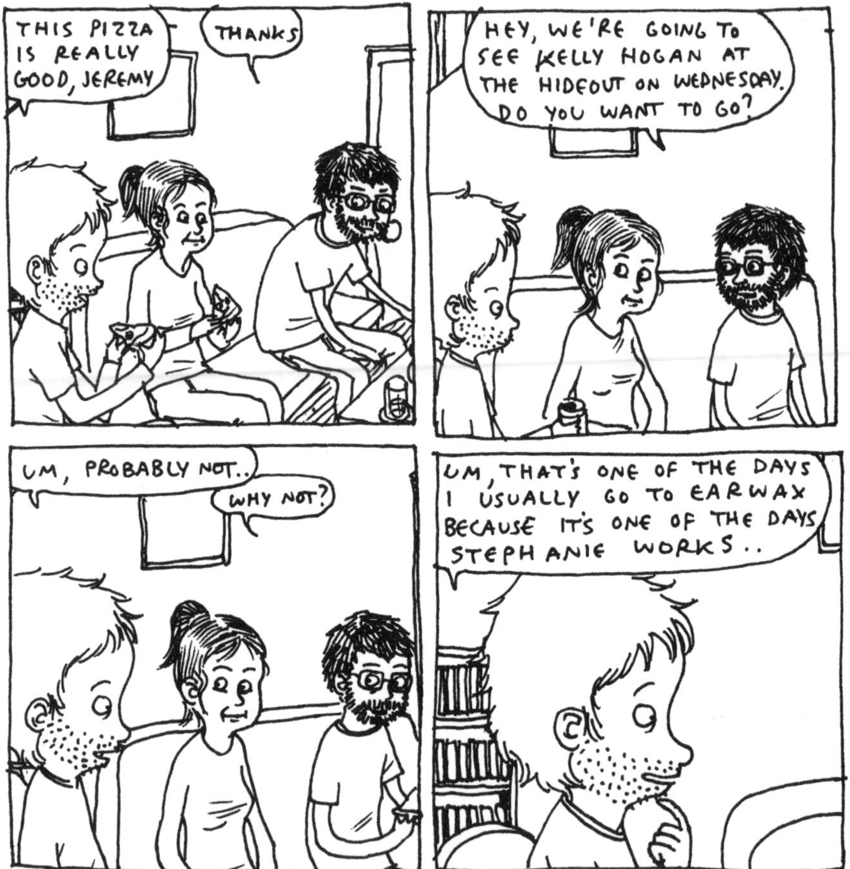
THIS PIZZA IS REALLY GOOD, JEREMY
THANKS
HEY, WE'RE GOING TO SEE KELLY HOGAN AT THE HIDEOUT ON WEDNESDAY. DO YOU WANT TO GO?
UM, PROBABLY NOT..
WHY NOT?
UM, THAT'S ONE OF THE DAYS I USUALLY GO TO EARWAX BECAUSE IT'S ONE OF THE DAYS STEPHANIE WORKS..

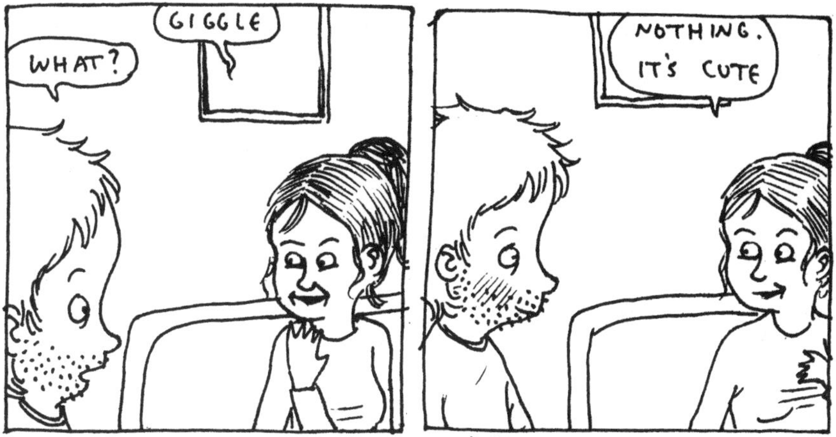
WHAT?
GIGGLE
NOTHING. IT'S CUTE

MONDAY

JANUARY 12

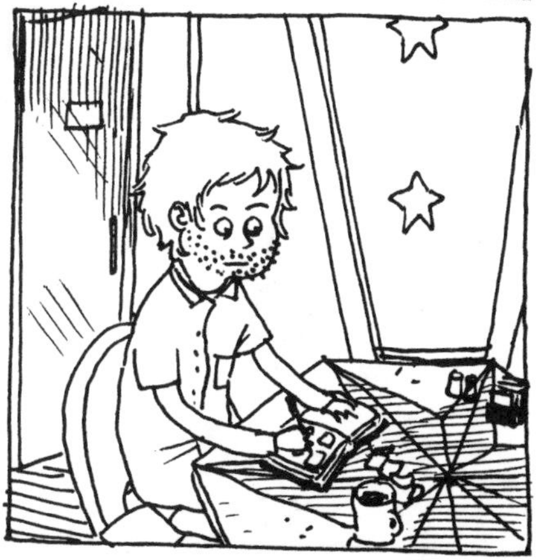

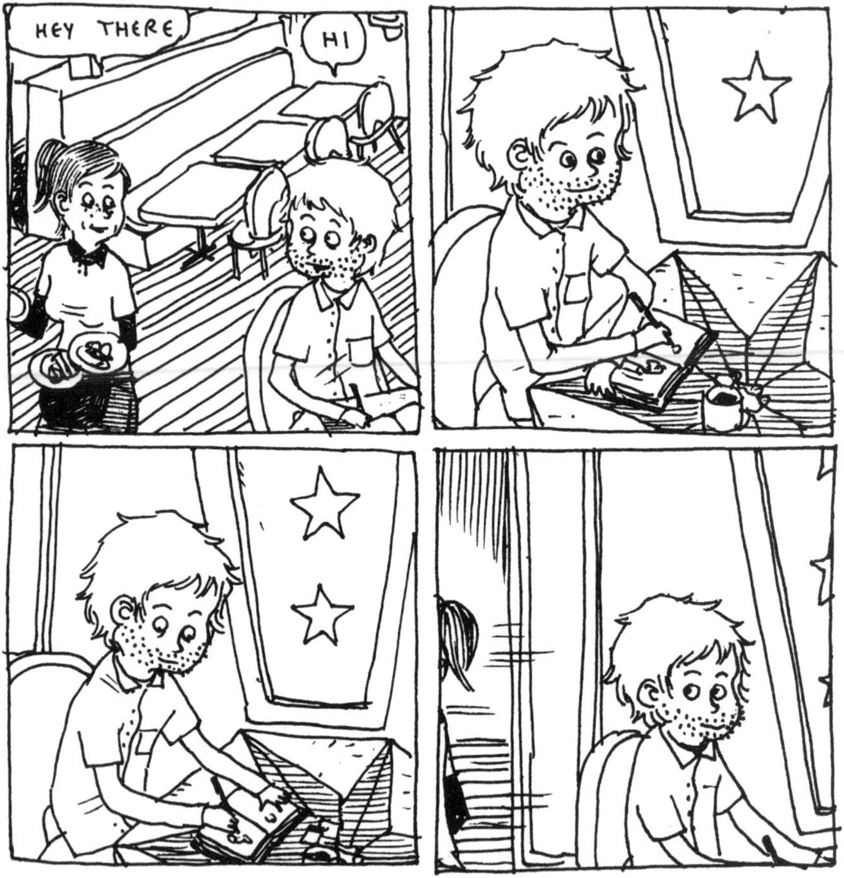
HEY THERE
HI

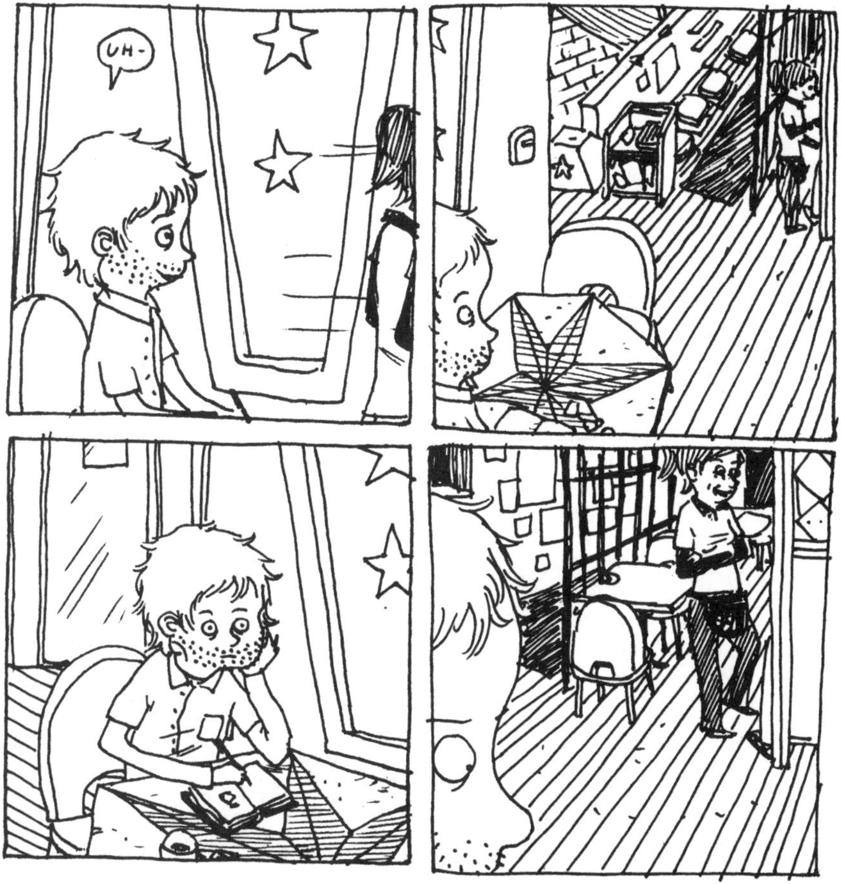
UH-

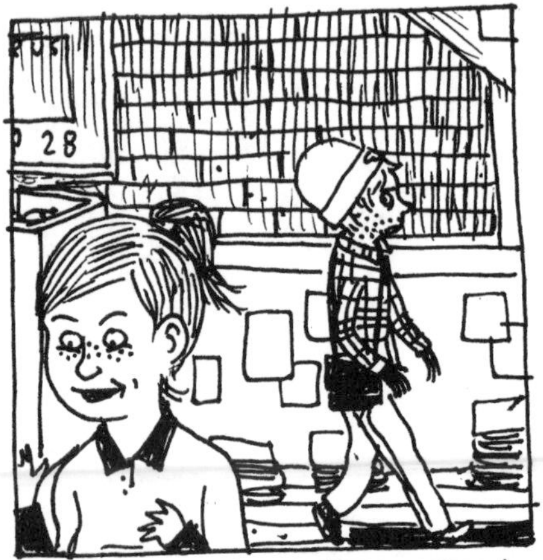
28

TUESDAY

JANUARY 13

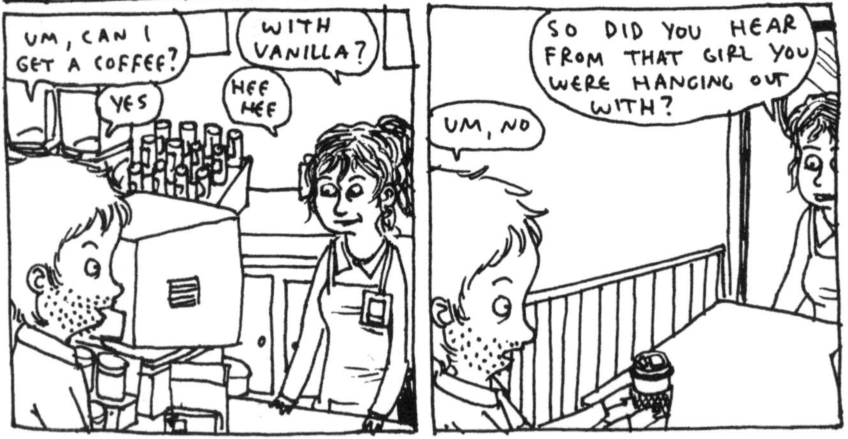
UM, CAN I GET A COFFEE?
YES
WITH VANILLA?
HEE HEE
SO DID YOU HEAR FROM THAT GIRL YOU WERE HANGING OUT WITH?
UM, NO

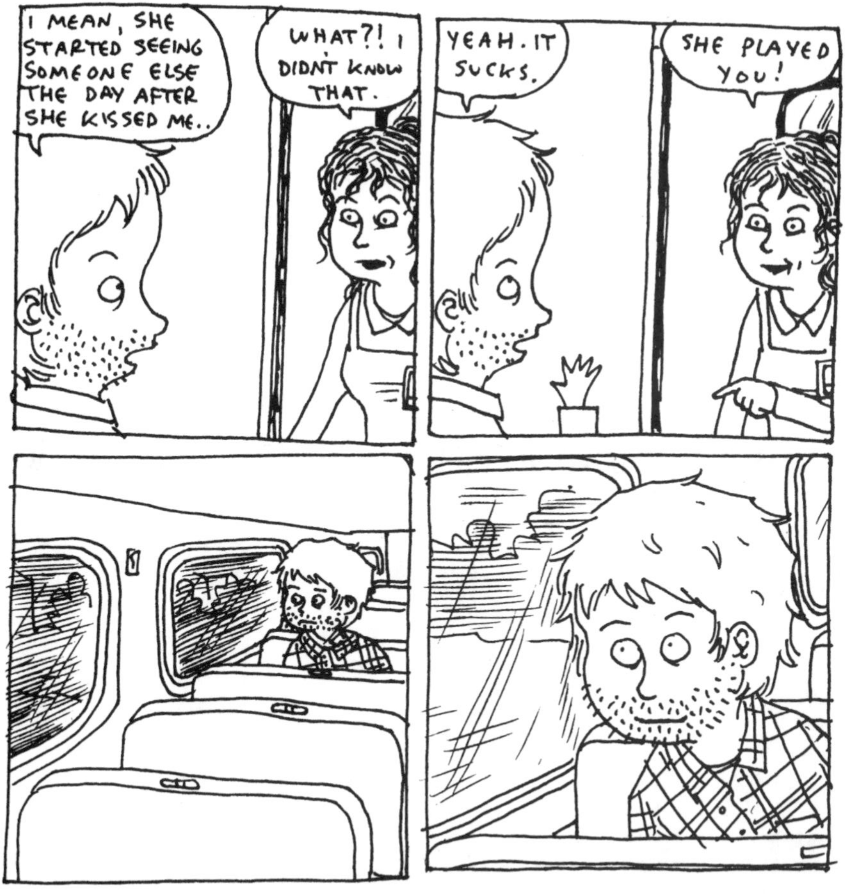
I MEAN, SHE STARTED SEEING SOMEONE ELSE THE DAY AFTER SHE KISSED ME..
WHAT?! I DIDN'T KNOW THAT.
YEAH. IT SUCKS.
SHE PLAYED YOU!

WEDNESDAY

JANUARY 14

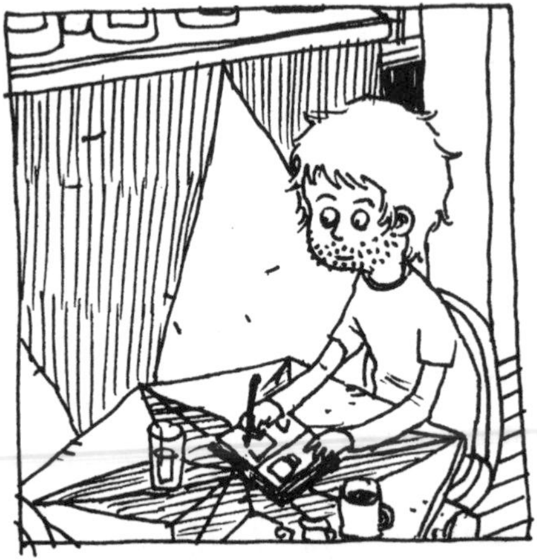

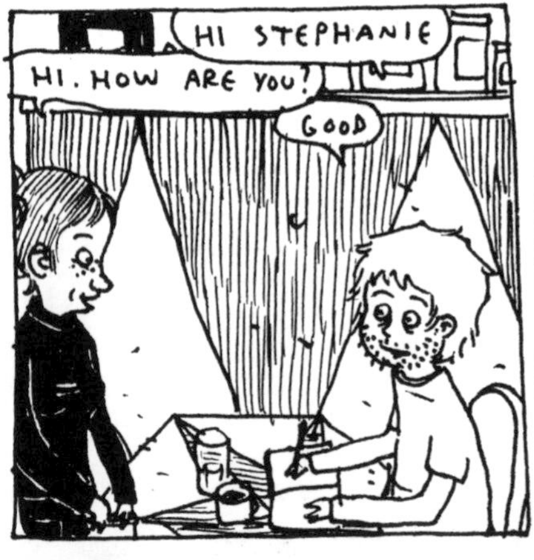
HI STEPHANIE
HI. HOW ARE YOU?
GOOD

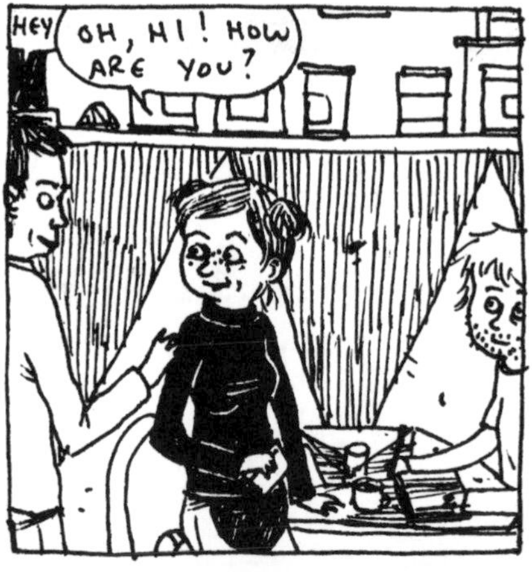
HEY
OH, HI! HOW ARE YOU?

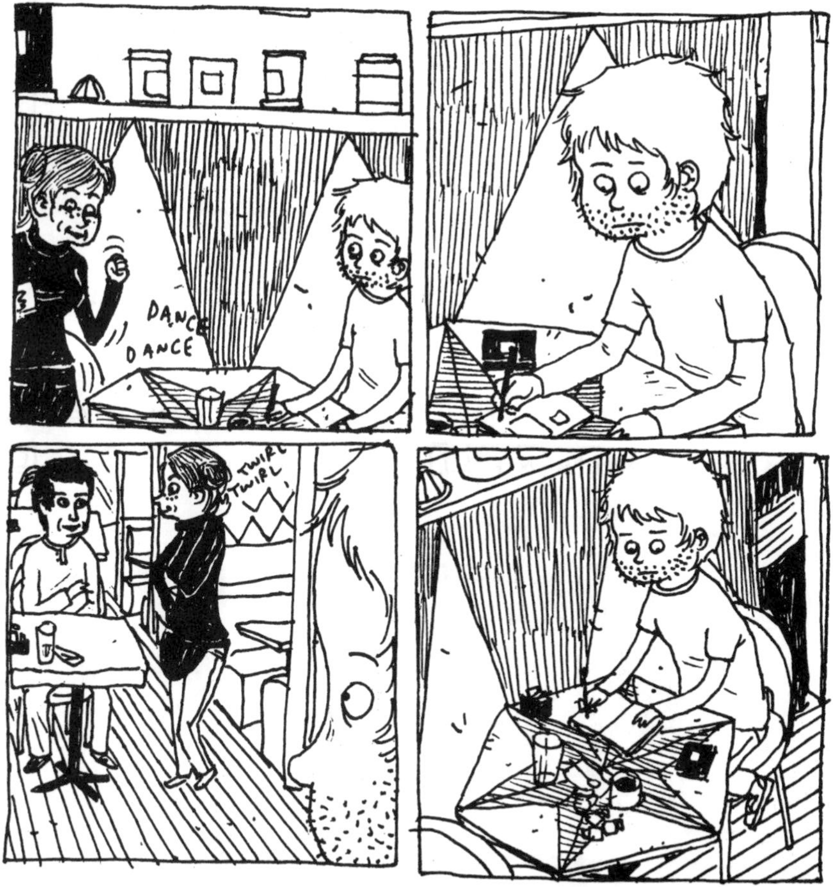
DANCE
DANCE
TWIRL
TWIRL

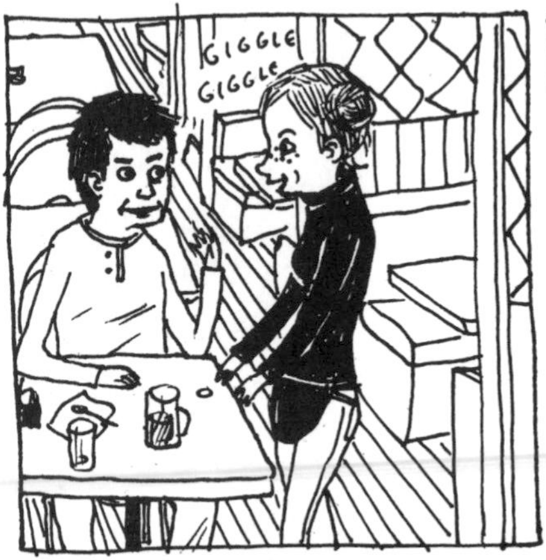
GIGGLE
GIGGLE

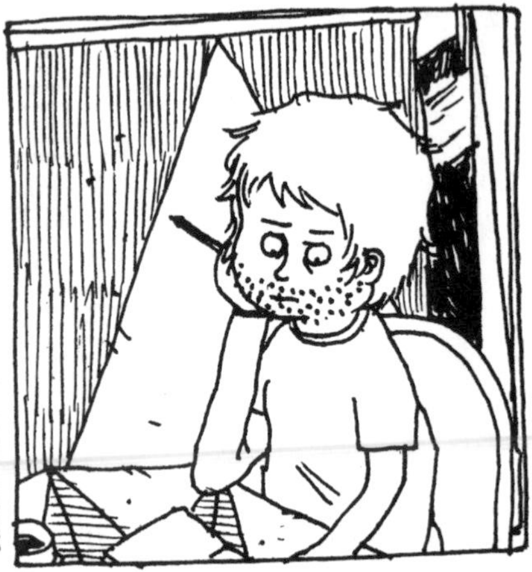

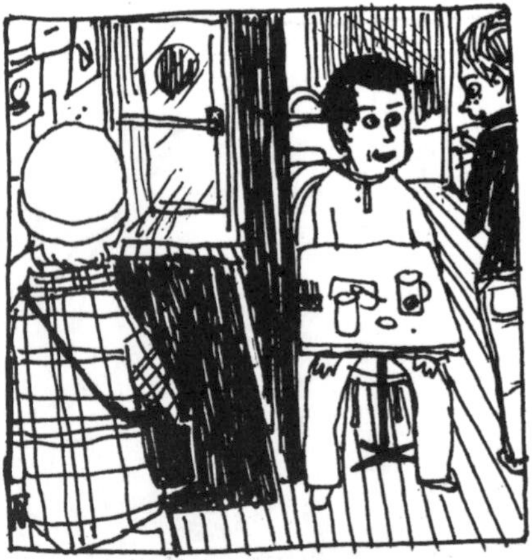

THURSDAY

JANUARY 15

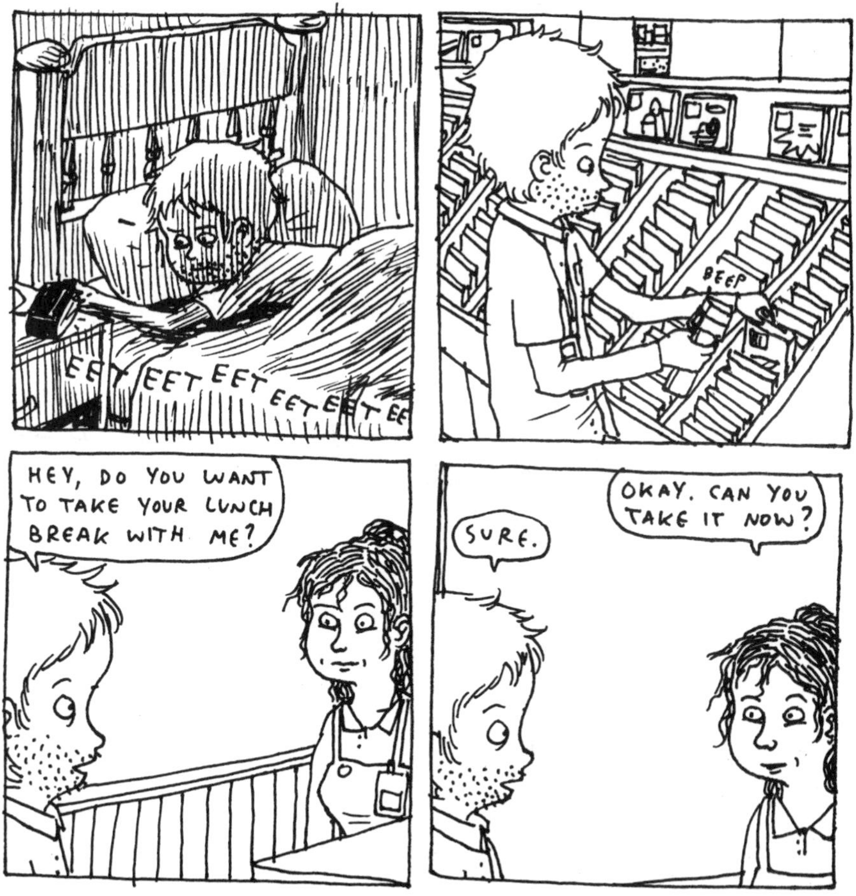
EET EET EET EET EET EET EE
BEEP
HEY, DO YOU WANT TO TAKE YOUR LUNCH BREAK WITH ME?
SURE.
OKAY. CAN YOU TAKE IT NOW?

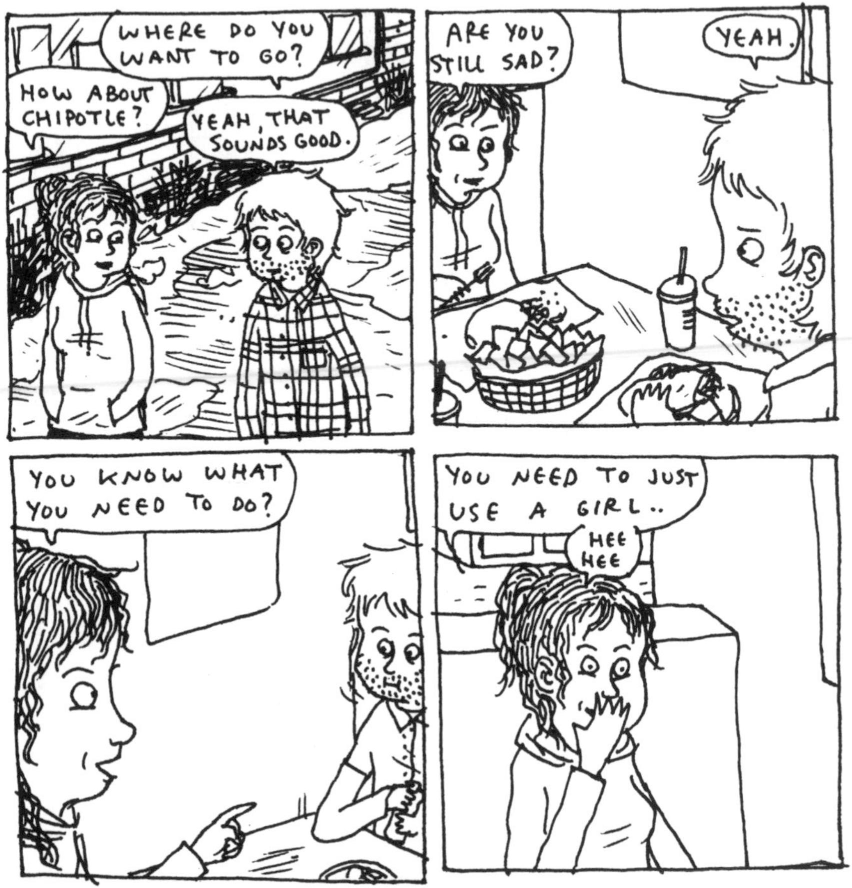
WHERE DO YOU WANT TO GO?
HOW ABOUT CHIPOTLE?
YEAH, THAT SOUNDS GOOD.
ARE YOU STILL SAD?
YEAH.
YOU KNOW WHAT YOU NEED TO DO?
YOU NEED TO JUST USE A GIRL..
HEE HEE

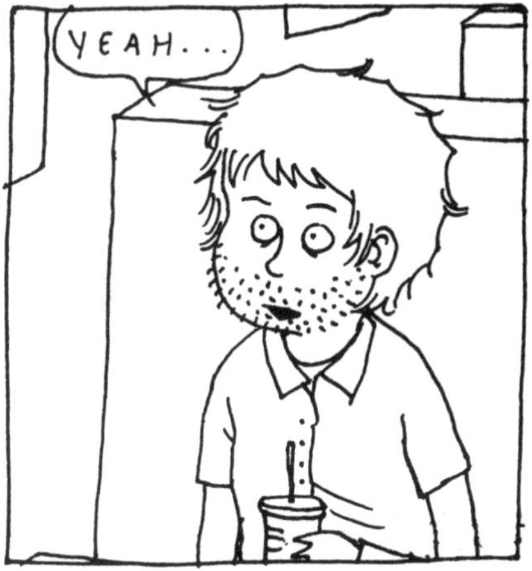
YEAH...

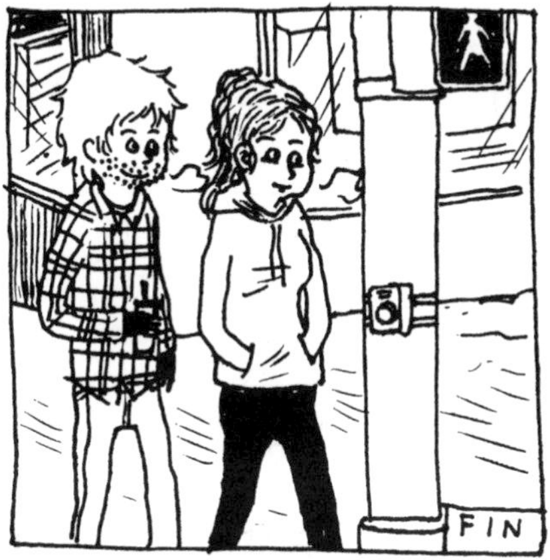
FIN

EPILOGUE

ONE YEAR LATER

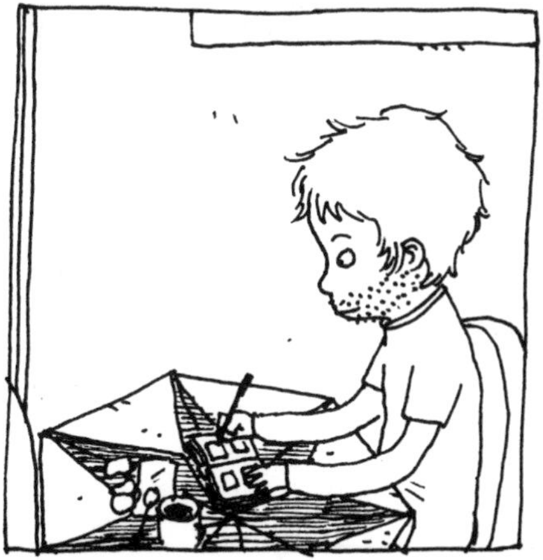

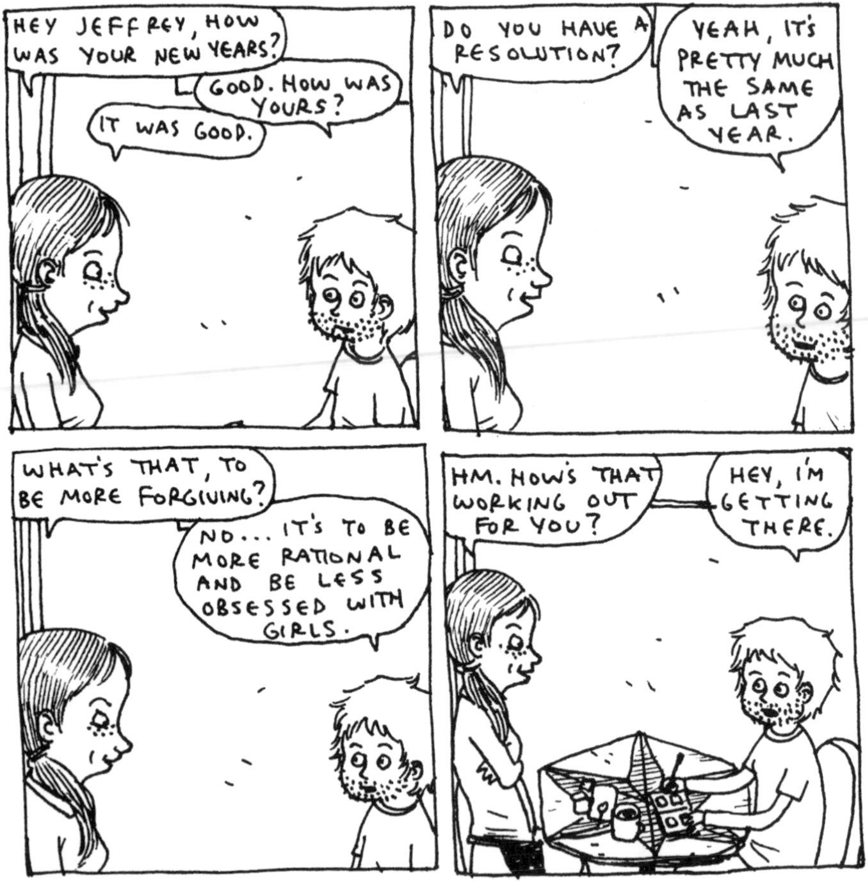
HEY JEFFREY, HOW WAS YOUR NEW YEARS?
GOOD. HOW WAS YOURS?
IT WAS GOOD.
DO YOU HAVE A RESOLUTION?
YEAH, IT'S PRETTY MUCH THE SAME AS LAST YEAR.
WHAT'S THAT, TO BE MORE FORGIVING?
NO... IT'S TO BE MORE RATIONAL AND BE LESS OBSESSED WITH GIRLS.
HM. HOW'S THAT WORKING OUT FOR YOU?
HEY, I'M GETTING THERE.

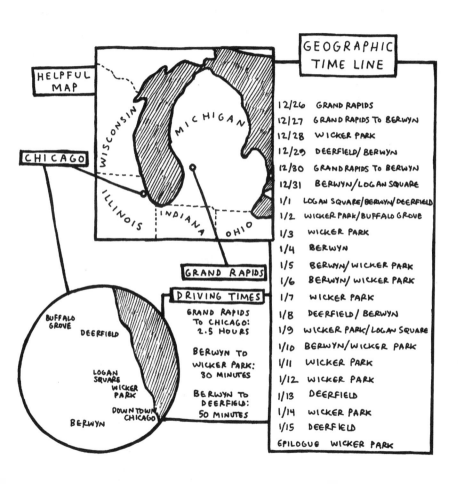

HELPFUL MAP

CHICAGO

WISCONSIN

MICHIGAN

ILLINOIS

INDIANA

OHIO

GRAND RAPIDS

BUFFALO GROVE

DEERFIELD

LOGAN SQUARE

WICKER PARK

DOWNTOWN CHICAGO

BERWYN

DRIVING TIMES

GRAND RAPIDS TO CHICAGO: 2.5 HOURS

BERWYN TO WICKER PARK: 30 MINUTES

BERWYN TO DEERFIELD: 50 MINUTES

GEOGRAPHIC TIME LINE

12/26   GRAND RAPIDS
12/27   GRAND RAPIDS TO BERWYN
12/28   WICKER PARK
12/29   DEERFIELD/BERWYN
12/30   GRAND RAPIDS TO BERWYN
12/31   BERWYN/LOGAN SQUARE
1/1   LOGAN SQUARE/BERWYN/DEERFIELD
1/2   WICKER PARK/BUFFALO GROVE
1/3   WICKER PARK
1/4   BERWYN
1/5   BERWYN/WICKER PARK
1/6   BERWYN/WICKER PARK
1/7   WICKER PARK
1/8   DEERFIELD/BERWYN
1/9   WICKER PARK/LOGAN SQUARE
1/10   BERWYN/WICKER PARK
1/11   WICKER PARK
1/12   WICKER PARK
1/13   DEERFIELD
1/14   WICKER PARK
1/15   DEERFIELD
EPILOGUE   WICKER PARK

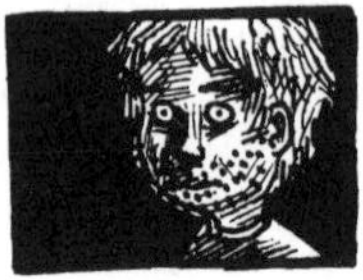

jeffreybrownrq@hotmail.com
P.O. BOX 120 Deerfield IL 60015
www.theholyconsumption.com

ALSO AVAILABLE BY JEFFREY BROWN:

CLUMSY

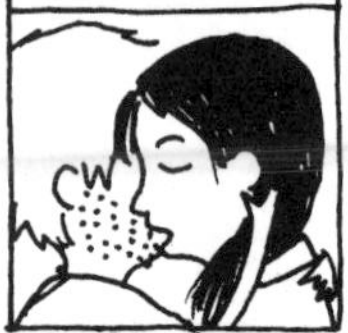

CW

232 PP. $10.00
STORY OF A LONG DISTANCE RELATIONSHIP

UNLIKELY

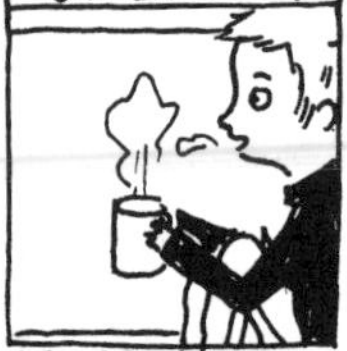

256 PP. $14.95
HOW I LOST MY VIRGINITY

AEIOU

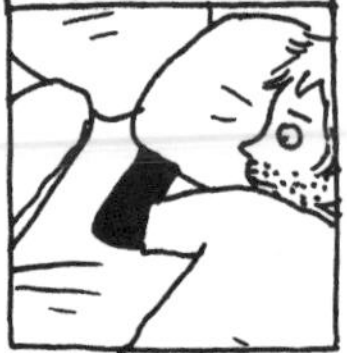

224 PP. $12.00
THIRD AND FINAL 'GIRLFRIEND' BOOK

BE A MAN

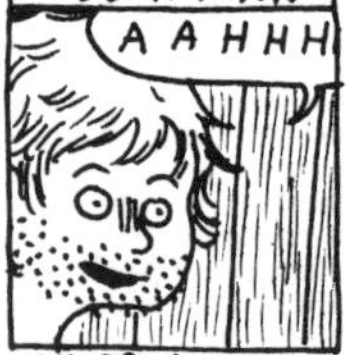

AAHHH

24 PP. $3.00
HILARIOUS PARODY OF 'CLUMSY'

MINISULK

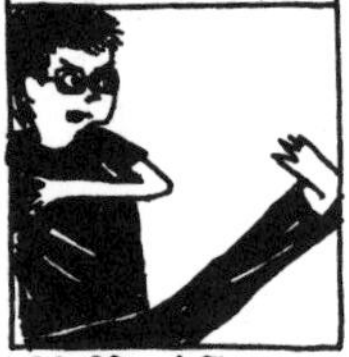

96 PP. $8.00
SHORT STORY AND GAG COLLECTION

BIGHEAD

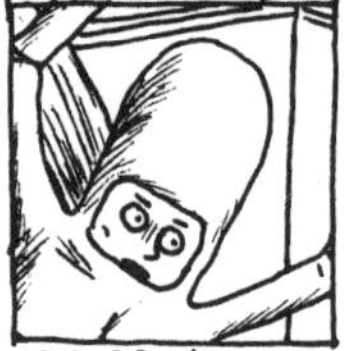

128 PP. $12.95
SUPER HERO PARODY

www.topshelfcomix.com